ECSTATIC BODY POSTURES

Ecstatic BODY POSTURES

An Alternate Reality Workbook

BELINDA GORE

FOREWORD BY
FELICITAS GOODMAN

BEAR & COMPANY
PUBLISHING
SANTA FE, NEW MEXICO

LIBRARY OF CONGRESS CATALOGING-IN-PUBLICATION DATA

Gore, Belinda.

    Ecstatic body postures : an alternate reality workbook / Belinda Gore ;
foreword by Felicitas Goodman.

         p.   cm.

    Includes bibliographical references.

    ISBN 1-879181-22-3 ; $20.00

    1. Trance. 2. Altered states of consciousness. 3. Posture in worship—
History. 4. Shamanism. I. Title.

    BF1045.A48G67 1995

    133—dc20   95-14892
                                           CIP

Bear & Company, Inc.
Santa Fe, NM 87504-2860

Cover design: Lightbourne Images
Interior page design and typography: Melinda Belter
Text illustrations: Patricia Stewart and Denise Satter
Editing: Gail Vivino
Printed in the United States of America by R. R. Donnelley

9 8 7 6 5 4 3 2 1

DEDICATION

To Felicitas Daniels Goodman—who is, above all, a wise, generous, and beloved friend. Her extraordinary scholarship, courageous vision, and personal dedication unveiled for us the treasure that lay right before our eyes.

And to the members of the Board of Directors and other friends of the Cuyamungue Institute, all fellow travelers in this great adventure. Those who made special contributions to the development of my understanding of the use of ecstatic body postures are Pamela Arden, Judy Field, MaryAnna Ireland, Robinette Kennedy, Carol Lang, Norma and Steve Leclair, Judy Morse, Jan Price, Elizabeth Russell, Linda Schroth, and Wendy Stone. My thanks to all of you.

CONTENTS

Foreword

Ecstatic Body Postures is an expanded and updated version of the handbook that Belinda Gore and I published as a manuscript three years ago under the label of Cuyamungue Institute. That manuscript in turn was based on my book *Where the Spirits Ride the Wind: Spirit Journeys and Ecstatic Experiences.* Its concise form and convenient layout, created by Belinda, gained it many friends, and it completely sold out. Thus we felt that it was time to take the next step and make it available to a wider readership. Belinda expanded and revised the original version and added a valuable psychological dimension, and we are grateful to Bear & Company, which is undertaking its publication.

In this foreword, I would like to give a summary of what our research is about. For those readers who are not familiar with our workshops, it may serve as an initial general orientation. Those who have already been part of our efforts may appreciate it as a refresher course and may also discover some new ideas that I, as the anthropologist on the team, have been able to develop over the course of the last few years.

What this book presents is a method for achieving ecstatic trance and its attendant visionary experiences. The method is based on my discovery that certain works of non-Western art—such as figurines and rock paintings—are not simply expressions of creativity, but in fact are ritual instructions. If a specific posture represented in one of these artifacts is combined with rhythmic stimulation, be that by drum or rattle, the body temporarily undergoes dramatic neurophysiological changes, and visionary experiences arise that are specific to the particular posture in question. In other words, whenever the same posture is assumed, the experience mediated is structured in a predetermined way. It is not a matter of automatic replication, as for instance would be the case with a computer-generated image. Rather, it is the framework that remains unaltered.

With one particular posture, for instance, we always take a trip to what shamans of old termed the Lower World. However, the manner in which we get there varies greatly: we may slip down through a tunnel, or turn a somersault, or arrive in many other ways, including simply and unexpectedly being "below." I recall one time turning into what seemed to be melted chocolate and gradually oozing down through a crack. Also, what we experience once we get there is subject to uncounted delightful variations. One of my more memorable encounters "down there" was with a vulture sitting on a rock wall next to a frightening chasm. As I shuddered looking down into the depth, the vulture grinned and put on a beaked cap.

The question arises, Where do we "go" when we "journey" in this manner? Do we explore our own inner worlds, or do we exit to another reality? The answer depends on each individual's background—his or her belief system, philosophical inclination, and worldview. As far as we at the Cuyamungue Institute are concerned, we present no "faith," only a particular kind of ecstatic experience. Adherents of many different convictions therefore feel comfortable in our workshops. As I was once prompted to point out to a gentle young nun, who had joined us out of curiosity and then became scared, "With us, tourists are always welcome." She did stay and had a good time. She later told us that she saw a figure she thought was the Virgin Mary, but when she looked closer, it turned out to be a tall, white bear. Specialists in these matters in the non-Western world—shamans, medicine people, priests, or whatever they might be called—all agree that what is contacted by way of religious ritual is Alternate Reality, a world "out there," the twin of the ordinary secular one, the sacred reality where the spirits dwell. In fact, the experiential contact with this part of reality is to my mind the very essence of what religion is about.

As our group at the Cuyamungue Institute has become more experienced and has experimented with larger numbers of postures, we have discovered that in order for a trance experience to be instituted, the posture has to be done exactly the way the "model"—the piece of art—presents it. If we are careless, or even if during a trance we change some feature of the posture—drop an arm or shift a leg—the experience disappears, much as an image leaves a television screen if the electricity goes out.

In Cuyamungue during the summer of 1994 we were doing the Lascaux Cave posture, which mediates a trip to the Upper World. All the participants managed to fly there except for one young woman, who, instead of rising to the world of rainbow clouds, only got a bad stomachache. It turned out that, with her being quite small, we had not noticed that as she had settled on the board that was inclined at the requisite 37-degree angle, she had turned her left arm the wrong way.

This observation and similar ones underscore the fact that the complex forms of the ritual postures are not some oddity, something we can play with as we please. The exact forms of these postures have been part of human religious observances from times immemorial. It is fascinating to note that the ritual postures share this feature of immutability with all other types of religious observances. Any religious ritual, be it a dance, song, play, possession, exorcism, or healing, must be done precisely as ordered, or, in traditional terms, the spirits will not react. In other words, the use of ritual body postures as a cultural trait is part of a venerable, ancient family of many different human behavior patterns.

We do not, of course, have any information about how these postures originated. Were they human inventions? I doubt it. Consider the fact that certain postures, for instance the Bear Spirit posture, arose almost simultaneously everywhere in the world during the sixth to fifth millennium before our time. That was a time when there was no modern method of communication whatsoever. The mythology of the non-Western world suggests a distinct method of propagation: the spirits invited humans, or in some instances actually "kidnapped" them, and taught them certain important rituals because humanity needed them.

In a subtle way, that is how our Masked Trance Dance ritual got its start, too. Early in the 1980s one of my Austrian friends conceived the notion that we should use the trance-posture experiences for "celebration." None of us had any idea how that could be done. In fact, he thought perhaps we could simply imitate some tribal ritual. To an anthropologist such as myself, the idea appeared preposterous. Native rituals are not only the inalienable property of the respective group, they are also deeply imbedded in the specific culture and language, and imitating them is patently impossible. So eventually I turned to the spirits for advice. We took a spirit journey to the Lower World in order to meet up with an animal spirit that wanted to be represented in a mask, and we did a divining posture so we would be instructed about the topic and details of a dance. The strategy was eminently successful. As a consequence, whenever we now do a Masked Trance Dance, this is how we proceed.

When I first discovered the ritual postures, most of the examples came from a few isolated societies and archaeological finds. I had no idea that we were dealing with a worldwide phenomenon. In fact, I reacted rather impatiently when friends began to point out that there were examples of our postures in museums and that they were derived from all sorts of places. Eventually, overwhelmed by the sheer volume of the material, I had to admit that they were right, and I began discovering that there was a certain order to this rich treasure trove. The artists who had created these magnificent pieces in fact belonged to only two types of societies: either hunting societies or horticulturalist societies—that is, societies that planted small gardens and also engaged in hunting or fishing. Other types of societies that we humans have evolved in the course of the long history of our species—the nomadic pastoralist societies, the agricultural societies, and the urban societies—were not represented. Nomadic pastoralists and agriculturalists, of course, also have certain poses that they assume during religious observances, but they are symbolic, and do not mediate entrance into Alternate Reality as an experience registered by some or all of the senses.

Of the above life ways, only the urban one did not develop its own type of religious ritual. Cities have tended through history to take on or conserve the religions of their hinterlands, so today there are horticulturalist cities such as Tokyo, Muslim cities like Teheran, and large numbers of agriculturalist cities on every continent. Cities, however, tend to dilute the traditional faiths; and the industrialized West especially has reduced religion to an intellectual, philosophical, or psychological exercise. Western city dwellers are typically ecstasy deprived, often turning to substitutes such as drugs to satisfy genetically anchored needs. The practice of ritual postures offers a way out of this dilemma. The participants in workshops are introduced to effective ways with which they can institute religious trance and structure meaningful experience with the help of the postures.

Ecstatic Body Postures offers advice on how to do postures either on your own or with a group. Of course, group experiences are more enjoyable, but so many of us simply do not have any community within which a posture session can be carried out. In fact, we are not only ecstasy deprived; we are also community deprived. Our communities tend to be tragically ephemeral. Even traditional families tend to dissolve as the children get older. In addition, workplaces keep changing, and neighborhoods are destroyed by development. However, as we work with the postures, spirit beings enter our lives and, in a subtle and very satisfying way, begin to fill the void. If we cannot have stable and lasting communities in ordinary reality, they can coalesce in Alternate Reality. I recall a woman in one of my workshops worrying about what would happen if, in addition to making friends with the Bear Spirit, as had already happened, she was now also interested in the Eagle Spirit. Would they be jealous of each other? When I pointed out that the Bear Spirit was a grandfatherly figure, her face lit up. "Oh," she exclaimed, "so he can actually be my grandfather and the eagle my older brother, and the snake whom I just saw, one of my sisters . . . ." In no time at all, and based on her various trance experiences, she had happily assembled an entire extended family.

So, with all this in mind, let me wish you much happy adventuring on the Path of the Spirits.

Felicitas D. Goodman, Ph.D.
Santa Fe, New Mexico
Fall 1994

Felicitas Goodman, Ph.D. is an anthropologist who taught for many years at Denison University in Granville, Ohio. She is the author of Where the Spirits Ride the Wind: Spirit Journeys and Ecstatic Experiences *and several other books. She currently lives in Columbus, Ohio, and teaches frequently at Cuyamungue Institute, near Santa Fe, New Mexico.*

Preface

This is the story of a great discovery and a story of hope for those of us living in the post-industrial age who are trying to find our roots and our way back home, hoping to find healing for our planet and for ourselves before it is too late.

The journey begins, as it must, with a personal story, for all discoveries, great and small, are revealed through the lives of ordinary people, some who have gifts of genius and others whose task it is to be at the right place at the right time. My part of this story begins in the fall of 1976, when I first began to record my dreams. I made a note in my journal about a dream of riding my bicycle to the house of a woman who was going to "teach me about the mysteries." Full of anticipation, I arrived at a white frame house with a white picket fence that was disappointingly small, and not in very good repair. Considering how grand an undertaking this seemed, I had expected something more magnificent. Nevertheless, I approached the front door, and a short gray-haired woman with piercing eyes opened the door and invited me to enter her house. She was welcoming and kind but refused to be the teacher I had expected. Instead, as I wrote in my journal, "she adopted me into a way of life."

My journal includes no other comments about this little dream. If I had been born into another culture, a culture that honored the visions of the Dreamtime, I would have taken my dream to the elders for help in understanding its meaning. As it was, I was a young counselor living in Ohio and studying metaphysics with a teacher in England. I had only begun to search my dreams for meaning, and while I believed that dreams could bring me messages from my own unconscious and from the realm of spirit, I was inexperienced in deciphering them. I could not have known that it would be another eight years before I would actually meet the gray-haired woman who lived in the white frame house, nor could I have imagined the world into which she would introduce me.

The woman's name was Felicitas Goodman, and I met her through my friend Anita. Anita had called one winter afternoon early in 1984 to tell me she had just had lunch with one of her former yoga students: "She's Hungarian, an anthropologist, and she plays the violin." On that recommendation alone, I accepted Anita's invitation to participate in a workshop that Dr. Goodman would be giving the following week at her home. My car was being repaired on the day the workshop began, so I rode the bus and walked up the street to the address I had been given. Because I walked I had time to notice, as I approached Dr. Goodman's house, that it was a small white frame house with a white picket fence. And as I walked through the gate and up the steps, Dr. Goodman herself, a small gray-haired woman of seventy years, met me at the door. I wish I could say that I recognized her at once from my dream, but I did not. I only knew that her cool, gray-brown eyes looked right into me, and when the workshop began and she told us her story, I felt as though some large piece of a puzzle slipped into place deep inside me.

Later I learned that it was in the fall of 1976, when I had first dreamed of her, that Dr. Goodman had made the discovery that is the substance of this book and that is the foundation for a way of life into which I, and many others, have been adopted. It is a magnificent way of life, yet simple, like the small white house I had seen in my dream.

The students of Dr. Goodman, who are practitioners of the body postures which she "discovered," wish to respect the sacred practices of indigenous peoples throughout the world. By sharing these ritual postures, I am not suggesting that they are the spiritual practices of any specific group of people. The specific preparations and rituals surrounding the use of the postures remain the private knowledge of the indigenous peoples. The postures themselves are not secret, however. The native artworks revealing these ritual postures have always been right in front of us, on cave walls, pottery, and totem poles. People are learning once again to use them, celebrating that what was lost is now found.

Ecstatic
BODY POSTURES

The Discovery

The religious specialists of small societies—medicine people, shamans, priests, and priestesses—have, for thousands of years, known and taught a sacred body of knowledge entrusted to them. Among these teachings are specialized techniques that open the door to a reality separate from the ordinary world. This Alternate Reality is known by many names and has been described by spiritual explorers throughout human history. The religious specialists have preserved the knowledge of this other world and the methods that allow us to alter ourselves so that we may slip through the crack between the worlds. They have known that this other reality is a constant source of wisdom and life-sustaining energy, and that it is good for humans to live in harmony with the world of spirits and to visit there often.

We have known about the practices of these religious specialists through the reports of anthropologists and ethnographers, stories that have come from their informants and from their own experiences of participating in ceremonial events. Some of these researchers have even been accepted as students and apprentices, learning the practices of particular teachers, groups, or societies. However, about fifteen years ago, Dr. Goodman stumbled onto a technique that is an essential ingredient of many traditions around the world that have existed from prehistoric times to the present. It is a spiritual tool that allows those of us living in the post-industrial technological age to safely enter the Alternate Reality known for thousands of years by medicine people of all traditions.

To appreciate Dr. Goodman's remarkable story, it is important to know the woman herself. She was born in the Hungarian part of Romania and was educated in Germany, where she was trained as a teacher and a scientific translator. Later she married an American professor and had four children. Eventually they moved from Germany to

Ohio, where her husband taught German at Ohio State University and she worked as a translator. It was not until 1965, at the age of 51, that she made a decision to pursue the investigative yearnings of her mind and heart. In her years as a scientific translator she had become proficient in a number of languages, so when she decided to return to the university, it made sense to her to undertake a masters degree in linguistics. But while linguistics was an intellectually challenging field, it did not satisfy the deeper longing that had led her to change the course of her life in the first place. Unexpectedly, that satisfaction came to her through an elective anthropology course taught by Dr. Erika Bourguignon entitled "Religion in Native Societies." It was here that she at last found the academic path she could wholeheartedly embrace.

With her proficiency in languages, Dr. Goodman was soon hired as a research assistant for Dr. Bourguignon, translating materials for a study funded by the National Institute of Mental Health that focused on behavior occurring during religious experience.[1] The purpose of the study was to systematically evaluate the religious trance state in 486 small societies to determine whether behavior labeled as psychotic by the standards of Western urban industrialized society is considered abnormal in a different cultural context. The outcome of this research clearly established that behaviors labeled by modern psychiatry as psychotic—such as seeing visions, hearing voices, and having contact with the dead—are not only considered normal but are institutionalized into the religious practices of 96 percent of the small societies that were studied. In these societies, non-consensual reality—that is, the experience of things and events not necessarily perceived by others at the same time and place—is accepted as normal. Indeed, it is those individuals who are *not* capable of altering their consciousness to perceive an alternate reality who are considered psychologically defective.

The experiences of a person in a religious altered state of consciousness—that is, perceiving Alternate Reality—are different from the symptoms of a person with a psychotic thought disorder. In the religious trance, there is a predetermined beginning and ending to each experience, and the individual returns to the ordinary state of consciousness with an intact self-aware ego. The person also emerges from trance with a sense of renewal and a message or other gift for the tribe or community, no matter how arduous the journey into the spirit realm has been. Psychosis, on the other hand, is unpredictable and unwanted, a madness that is both disorienting and lacking in meaning in ordinary reality. The ability to begin and end an altered state of consciousness on cue and the sense of meaning and fulfillment that follow the experience are the criteria used to distinguish madness from spiritual ecstasy.

Some might say that it was coincidental that Dr. Goodman became involved in Dr. Bourguignon's research project, since the outcome of this research established a conceptual foundation for Dr. Goodman's later work. However, there were many other coincidences or strokes of fate that would guide her toward her most important discovery, which is the substance of this book. She identified that her real love was not linguistics but the study of religious and psychological anthropology. While she was still a doctoral student, she was offered a collection of audiotapes that students and colleagues of Dr. Bourguignon had accumulated during their fieldwork. These tapes were recordings, from all over the world, of the phenomenon called "glossolalia," more commonly known as "speaking in tongues." Using her training as a linguist, she set out to investigate whether or not glossolalia followed the rules of a language in terms of structure and vocabulary. Her conclusion, which she published in a small volume[2] that is still one of the definitive studies in the field, was that glossolalia is not a language in the formal sense, but rather a vocalization that accompanies the physiological changes occurring during a specialized state of consciousness known as the religious trance state. Also called the ecstatic trance state, this altered state of consciousness can be achieved through a set of specialized conditions and a rhythmic stimulation of the nervous system.

In the small, charismatic, apostolic churches where she did her own fieldwork in the Yucatan, Dr. Goodman observed again and again the methods that ministers used to teach their congregations how to enter this religious altered state. Ecstatic or religious trance was necessary in order for a parishioner to receive the Holy Spirit; hence it was a requirement for the salvation of each member of the congregation. These ministers were experts at leading people through the steps necessary to achieve a trance state, even though most of them would probably have been outraged at the suggestion that they were teaching anyone to go into a trance. In these fundamentalist churches, being visited by the Holy Spirit would not have been considered an ecstatic trance state, even though that is exactly what it was. Nevertheless, these ministers knew subtle yet obvious means for leading their congregations into a special state in which they could receive the Holy Spirit and speak in tongues.

Upon returning to her teaching position at Denison University in Ohio, Dr. Goodman used the same techniques to teach her student volunteers to alter their states of consciousness and achieve a similar trance state. This was the early 1970s, and her students were no strangers to alternative states of consciousness, having experimented with hallucinogenic drugs, meditation, and other spiritual practices based in Eastern religions. They were eager to explore and learn, so for several years Dr. Goodman used the methods she had learned in the apostolic churches to teach them how to enter the religious trance state.

Some of the conditions necessary for achieving the trance state were so obvious that they might have been overlooked by a less astute observer. For instance, Dr. Goodman identified the need for participants to be in a private physical space separate from the comings and goings of everyday living. Therefore, she replicated the little church in the Yucatecan village where she did her fieldwork in a carpeted classroom at the university. It was quiet there, and her student volunteers were not interrupted during the trance. Additionally, Dr. Goodman knew it was

necessary for the participants to come to the experience with an expectation of a nonordinary state of consciousness. It was important for them
to believe that what they would be doing would be both normal—that is,
not crazy—and enjoyable, something to be anticipated with openness and
pleasure.

Another requirement for the trance state was a technique to assist the
participants' concentration. This would help shift the focus of their
minds from classes and the ordinary events of life. In the Yucatecan
church, the minister fulfilled this requirement by having the people sing
hymns and by exhorting them to leave behind the everyday world. This
requirement was initially overlooked with the Denison students, however.
Only in Dr. Goodman's later research was a simple breathing exercise,
inspired by meditation techniques, recommended. Even then people were
simply instructed to count their breaths. They were not told to use hatha
breaths or diaphragmatic breathing, but simply to notice the air as it
entered their nostrils and then gently release it.

Each inhalation/exhalation cycle counted as one breath. Fifty such
breaths took about five minutes. In that time, if the participants kept
bringing their thoughts back to their breathing, to following the air in and
out of their nostrils, then their bodies quieted and their minds were ready
to focus. While this technique was similar to meditation, Zen practitioners found it especially difficult to open up to the experience of ecstatic
trance because they had trained themselves to continuously empty their
minds. The concentration exercise is only for focus; in trance, the mind
becomes receptive to perceptions from nonordinary reality and no longer
should remain empty.

The final component to achieve the trance state was some kind of
rhythmic stimulation of the nervous system. In the Yucatecan church, it
was the singing and clapping of hands, rhythmically and repetitively. This
singing and clapping had a hypnotic effect. At Denison, Dr. Goodman
brought in a gourd rattle like those commonly made by the Pueblo

Indians in the American Southwest. These rattles are made from dried gourds hollowed out and partially filled with the tiny stones that ants bring up from beneath the surface of the land. By tradition, these stones are pure, uncontaminated by human activity in the world. When the gourd rattle is shaken, the stones make a sharp, distinctive sound.

Using a consistent rhythm of 210 beats per minute, Dr. Goodman would rattle for fifteen minutes. In her early experiments, she found that people reported feeling unfinished when the rattling was limited to ten minutes, and that if she rattled for longer than fifteen minutes, people were either exhausted or reported empty time toward the end of the rattling period. So fifteen minutes became the standard. The rattling sound cued the participants' bodies to shift into an alternate mode of perception. Drumming and other similarly complex, reverberating sounds can have the same effect.

Dr. Goodman's early experiments with her Denison students were interesting, but the outcomes were disappointing. While almost all of the students were able to achieve some altered state of functioning, there was no consistency among their experiences. Perhaps, Dr. Goodman concluded, the religious ecstatic trance required a shared dogma—a consistent worldview that would shape the experience. The students definitely had inner visual and auditory perceptions and could feel changes in their bodies, but without a common mythology to bind the perceptions, it seemed as though they were wandering aimlessly in altered states of consciousness. This was no different from random excursions with hallucinogenic drugs. She laid the investigation to rest, her sense of possibilities unfulfilled.

Months later, Dr. Goodman discovered an article by Canadian psychologist V.F. Emerson[3] on the subtle changes in body functioning—galvanic skin response, hormone secretion, blood pressure—that result from altered body posture or position. He had examined differences in these metabolic measurements as a result of varied meditation positions. Inspired, Dr. Goodman considered that the posture of the body might affect a person's overall experience of the trance. After all, the basic structure of the human body and its nervous system was universal and had changed very little over recent history. The human body was something all people shared in common, despite their religious beliefs or lack of them. Could body posture shape the altered state created by anticipation, concentration, and rhythmic stimulation of the nervous system? Perhaps this was the factor that was missing.

Dr. Goodman began to review the ethnographic literature for examples of artwork from indigenous peoples around the world that depicted body postures. She chose those which she thought might be related to religious experience. Some of the drawings, pottery, and carvings were accompanied by written text that suggested they were related to spiritual practices. Others, like a Pacific Northwest carving of a shaman with a huge bear embracing him from behind, revealed a connection with religious trance in the context and facial expressions of the little figures holding these special poses.

In 1977, Dr. Goodman began more controlled experiments using the postures now known as the Nupe Mallam, the Bear Spirit, the Lascaux Cave, the Singing Shaman, and the Aborigine Bone-Pointing postures. She examined the effects of combining specific postures with the necessary preliminary conditions for religious trance and the rhythmic auditory stimulation of the rattling. To control the unwanted influences of a group setting, she worked with individuals, recording their reports and comparing them, searching for patterns. She found what she was hoping for. Within a fairly wide range of individual variability, there was a clear indication that each posture provided a distinctive experience in trance—an undeniable pattern. Admittedly, the earliest indicators were vague. In the Bear Spirit posture, for instance, almost all participants became very hot, and many saw shades of blue. In the posture from the walls of the Lascaux cave in southern France, people reported feeling as if they were moving up and out of their bodies, and they often saw birds or experienced flying.

Most significant, however, was the deep emotional quality of the experiences reported by her research subjects at the conclusion of their fifteen minute trances. What they saw and heard often moved them to tears or profound joy. Their experiences held meanings for them that were sometimes inexpressible, taking them beyond the boundaries of their ordinary understanding. Dr. Goodman later wrote, "Guided by hitherto unnoticed traditional body postures, these 'subjects' of a social-science experiment had taken the step from the physical change of the trance to the experience of ecstasy; they had passed from the secular to the sacred."[4] They had had religious experiences.

It is remarkable that an alteration in body posture can have such a profound effect. There is a variety of other well-known physical techniques for inducing trance. Fasting is an ancient and well-respected tool. Many traditions use hallucinogenic plants or carefully measured substances that are toxic to the body to induce altered states. Middle Eastern priestesses and Native American medicine people have been taught as apprentices to tolerate snake venom in order to induce their spiritual trances. Self-flagellation was a favored tool among some monastic orders, and other forms of intense pain have been part of initiation rites in various cultures. Fortunately, the simple auditory stimulation of rattling, clapping, or drumming can have a similar effect. Multiple sound frequencies recurring at an even, steady rate are believed to block the left-hemisphere processing of the cerebral cortex and simultaneously to stimulate the peripheral nervous system.[5] The combined effect is the safe induction of an altered state of consciousness. While the other methods named above induce significant stress in the physical body, rattling or drumming can be used without risk to those who have not been prepared since early childhood for trance and who do not have the supervision of a shaman or other highly trained and experienced spiritual guide.

Physiological changes alone do not produce the religious experience, however. Ecstasy requires ritual to mediate the trance state. Ritual is the key factor that translates the physiological experience of trance into ecstasy. Forms of ritual are embedded in the sacred traditions of almost every culture throughout history. Many are very elaborate, and some are carefully guarded secrets. The beauty of the ritual postures is that each posture is itself a ritual, and it is a ritual with such exquisite precision and strength that it accomplishes its purpose outside the context of culture. A group of post-modern city dwellers can therefore successfully accomplish a traditional spirit journey with only simple drumming, a few simple preparatory conditions, and a spirit journey posture such as the one used by the shaman of the Lascaux cave, for example.

Subjectively, the ecstatic trance alters our perceptual abilities, tuning out the world of the ordinary senses and making us receptive to stimulation from what has been called nonordinary reality, Alternate Reality, or the "nagual," to use the term Carlos Casteneda learned from his teacher, don Juan. The existence of this other reality has been known throughout time. Black Elk, the Lakota medicine man whose visions were documented by John Neihardt, spoke of "the world where there is nothing but the spirits of all things. This is the real world that is behind this one, and everything we see here is something like a shadow from that world."[6] This description is similar to Plato's analogy of humans as prisoners in a cave, wrongly believing that the shadows on the wall before them are the only reality. When the prisoners' chains are broken, they are at last able to turn around to see the source behind the shadow, which is the true reality. Albert Hoffman, the Swiss chemist who discovered LSD, speaks in similar terms of his chemically induced altered state: "What impressed me most in my self-experiments with LSD . . . was the feeling I had of entering another reality. This other reality was experienced as quite real, even more than everyday reality."[7]

In order to perceive this other reality, we must be able to alter our bodies' functioning. As we learn to use the ritual body postures, we also train the nervous system to alter its functioning. After the preparatory breathing exercise, and once the rattling or drumming begins, the body undergoes changes that are characteristic of the ecstatic trance state. The research of Dr. Ingrid Mueller[8] at the University of Munich offers us a composite picture of the physiological changes that occur during the ecstatic trance state. The blood levels of the stress-related hormones cortisol, epinephrine, and norepinephrine initially rise, then drop dramatically during the course of the standard fifteen-minute trance. At the same time, the brain synthesizes beta-endorphins, which are responsible for the signature feeling of well-being that makes trance so appealing. The blood pressure drops, but at the same time the pulse rate increases, a rare combination usually associated with the preliminary stages of dying. Shamans have often said that they die during trance, and these data suggest that they were well aware of what we consider to be sophisticated knowledge of physiology.

Dr. Mueller's overall findings are consistent regardless of the subject's level of experience with trance or the specific posture used. None of the other altered states that have been studied, such as hypnotic trance, REM and non-REM sleep, and meditation, has this characteristic combination of effects.

In addition, during the ecstatic trance the brain waves pulse at the theta level, about six to seven cycles per second, usually associated with deep sleep or the meditative state achieved by accomplished Zen practitioners. At the University of Vienna, Professor Giselher Guttmann has developed a technology for measuring brain waves by direct current rather than alternating current. In a state of normal concentration, subjects register brain waves of about 100 microvolts; during ecstatic trance, individuals with some experience in ecstatic trance record brain waves of 1000 to 2500 microvolts.[9] Something clearly happens in the brain during trance that extends our normal capacities beyond what we can imagine.

All of this information indicates that the body undergoes tremendous change during periods of ecstatic trance. Nevertheless, Dr.

Goodman's research with over a thousand subjects has determined that anyone with a normally functioning nervous system can shift easily into ecstatic trance on cue, and just as easily, on cue return to the ordinary state of consciousness. Not only are inexperienced individuals able to learn how to enter the ecstatic trance state easily, but Dr. Goodman suggests that the nervous system periodically needs to be exercised in this way.

Without the opportunity to regularly alter our bodies and our consciousness in a religious trance, we experience what Dr. Goodman calls "ecstasy deprivation." We live in a society devoid of trance as a regular aspect of our spiritual lives. Many of us living in agricultural and urban settings react unconsciously to this absence of bliss and turn to alternative measures for achieving modified ecstasy. The well-documented addictive behavior that is becoming the psychological hallmark of our contemporary culture is evidence of our collective attempt to fill the emptiness created by our ecstasy deprivation. We eat too much of foods that are bad for us, exercise compulsively, and use alcohol, drugs, caffeine, nicotine, work, or sex to relieve the gnawing hunger for bliss.

What has happened to us culturally that we have become so removed from our lineage of spiritual ecstasy which extends back beyond recorded human history? In order to understand the problem, it is necessary to put our culture in the context of the development of human societies.

Until forty thousand years ago, all humans lived in cultures with a hunter-gatherer lifestyle. Dr. Robinette Kennedy, who is actively involved in the Cuyamungue Institute's research on ritual body postures, is among the contemporary feminist anthropologists who suggest that the term *hunter gatherers* be changed to the term *gathering hunters*. Among gathering-hunter societies, which still survive on several continents, it is primarily the women's gathering activity that sustains these wandering groups. Their diets of roots, nuts, fruits, and berries were initially supplemented by snared birds, small game, and what the men could scavenge. Much later, these people learned how to hunt large game, and then some groups became chiefly meat eaters.

In popular literature, there are some wonderful stories that invite us to understand this way of life on the planet when all human beings lived by gathering and hunting. One of my favorites is *Reindeer Moon*, a novel by anthropologist Elizabeth Marshall Thomas.[10] Thomas tells the story of a young woman's life in a tribe thousands of years ago, somewhere where the winters were dark and cold, and the summertime green. In the novel the woman eventually dies and becomes a spirit for her tribe, sometimes a wolf and sometimes a woman. The gathering-hunting way of life continues today: Richard Katz's fine book *Boiling Energy*,[11] describing the Kung of sub-Saharan Africa, and Marlo Morgan's fictionalized journey with the Australian Aborigines, recounted in her book *Mutant Message*,[12] are modern examples of this way of living and relating to the environment.

The boundaries between human beings and animal beings were thin in ancient times, and the traditions of most gathering hunters include stories of communication with animals. There is, for instance, a story from the Pacific Northwest of a fisherman who, in his search for new fishing grounds, paddled his kayak into an unknown bay. Wanting to discover more about this curious place, he brought his small boat onto the sandy beach and set off on foot. After he had walked a while, he began to hear uproarious laughter and cautiously followed the sound until it led him to the mouth of a cave. Careful not to be discovered, he crept through the darkness. Finally he arrived at the edge of a huge cavern. Gathered around a great roaring fire were animals of all varieties, large and small, playing a game that made them laugh so gloriously. It was the game of shapeshifting, in which they changed their bodies, heads, and limbs into those of human beings, then laughed in delight at the comedy of forms they created.

The lifeway of gathering hunters is characterized by balance and harmony with the natural world—not just with animals but with all life forms, including wind and thunder, rocks and insects. Humans are not thought of as having dominion over the Earth or any of its inhabitants, and so gathering hunters are not focused on attempts to control their environment, but rather on living in harmonious relationship with the seasons, the elements, and all living beings. This attitude is so effective and adaptive that gathering and hunting existed as the only way of life on our planet for thousands of years.

Spirit journeys are an inherent part of the religious practices of the gathering hunters. From a contemporary perspective, spirit journeys might be considered similar to out-of-body experiences, although spirit journeying is an experience that is deeply connected with the body rather than dissociated from it. When the appropriate physiological cues are activated, it becomes possible to attune to an alternative set of organs of perception and to shift into a spirit body capable of witnessing and participating in the spirit world. Within the worldview of the hunter gatherers, the spirit journey is the primary religious experience during which it is possible to descend into the Lower World or Underworld of the animal spirits and the dead, to travel across the Middle World that is the spirit counterpart of ordinary reality, or to soar into the Sky World or Upper World, which is the home of the Cloud Beings and Thunder Beings, the Sun and Moon and the star nations.

The roots of the Tree of Life are nourished by the soil of the Lower World, and so are the roots of the human psyche. The Lower World is home to the animal spirits, whom the gathering hunters recognize as older and wiser brothers and sisters, capable and willing to serve as guides to humans. Each animal spirit is known to have certain special qualities and knowledge that are shared with humans when sought in a respectful and sacred way. A spirit journey to the Lower World is generally undertaken either to find an animal friend and ally or to seek the help and counsel of one or more animal spirits. The journey may be grueling or delightful, but the basic purpose is to find guidance and solutions.

The Lower World or Underworld is also the Realm of the Dead, the place to which human spirits travel after physical death. In the Realm of the Dead, a human spirit experiences loss of personal identity with the physical body, sometimes being reduced to bones and ash before taking a spirit form and rising to another world. The Realm of the Dead may be perceived as a macabre place, brimming with decay and loss, or as a place of rest.

Spirit journeying in the Middle World has several functions. It provides a means of travel and communication without cars, airplanes, satellite dishes, or fiber-optic networks. It is a means of scanning territory to find the location of medicinal herbs or game, to discover the presence of intruders, or to establish vital communication links with people at great distances. In some cases, it can provide recreation for people who withdraw for long winters without benefit of books or movies or vacations.

Gathering hunters go to the Sky World to find ways to restore balance in the world. Healing in the world of the gathering hunters is defined as the restoration and maintenance of balance. It is understood that the activities of humans, exercising their abilities to make reasoned rather than instinctual choices, cause imbalance. However, it is also within the capacity of humans to interact with Alternate Reality and enact rituals to restore the natural order that has been disrupted. One task of the shaman is to guide this process of healing by making spirit journeys to the Sky World.

It is a powerful lesson to realize that today, when we are at the brink of ecological disaster, it is within our human power to enact rituals that can help bring the natural world back into harmony. A few years ago, as part of an ecstatic trance workshop, I experienced, in trance, the agonizing destruction of Earth by fire. Overcome with pain and grief over all I had witnessed and felt, I arrived at a spot where there was a gathering of animal spirits. Seeing my despair, they beckoned me to come look through the mists, down upon Earth where our preparations for the concluding ceremony of our workshop were underway. "See," they said, "all is not lost. The humans down there are doing their part." Through that experience I realized that even a small group of relative neophytes could make a difference in a world in which the elders who had traditionally kept order were dwindling in number, their people and ways of life shaken by urban industrialization.

Change in lifeways affected the hunters of Neolithic times. Hunter gatherers require about one square mile per person per year to provide a tribe with enough food without denuding the habitat. As populations grew, there was an increased need for food. The women in their seasonal rounds of gathering had learned about the life cycles of plants. They began to plant seeds or possibly transplant roots and cultivate small gardens. Over time, some groups grew to rely primarily on their gardens, such as the Pueblo Indians of today who raise corn, beans, and squash as their main sources of food. This change from gathering and hunting to cultivating food led to a significant change in lifestyle. Mobility declined as it became necessary to stay in the vicinity of the gardens. People began to live together in communities rather than tribes, and social relationships began to change. Individualism lost importance as the need to live together in restricted spaces grew.

In this process of controlling the natural cycles of plants and regulating their own social interactions, the people in horticultural societies seemed to lose the deep sense of unity with the natural world that had characterized their hunter-gathering ancestors. In their spiritual practices, however, these horticulturalists were able to restore this connection through what is referred to in this book as "metamorphosis trance." Through metamorphosis trance it was possible to soften the boundaries between humans, animals, and plants, and to return, however briefly, to a state of being at one with the others. The use of ritual body postures was developed within horticultural societies. These were the peoples who refined the use of body postures as rituals that gave shape to religious trance. Dr. Goodman discovered that they passed along to us a well-defined system that teaches us how to enter Alternate Reality, the spirit world, where we can return to a state of harmony with the four-leggeds, those that fly, those that swim, the plants, the trees, and the rocks.

As the land became more and more populated, diversification increased. Some people no longer hunted or raised their own food at all, and others undertook large-scale agriculture. The illusion of power and control over the natural world increased, and the split between humans and animals deepened. Duality became the focus in spiritual and secular visioning of the world. This world of ordinary reality and the spirit world were split between good and evil, heaven and hell, above and below, spirit and body, God and the Devil. There developed hierarchical systems of defining power in relationships, the domestication of animals, the ownership of land and animals and people, a belief that one finds God by going "up," and the concept that holiness is found in denying the body. Experiences in Alternate Reality were described either in terms of surrender or grace, meaning giving up control, or in terms of possession—being overtaken by the Holy Spirit, other "good" spirits, or by demons.

Agriculturalists lost the knowledge of ritual body postures as doorways to the world of spirits. The postures no longer appeared in any art forms of these cultures. It is curious, then, that the way back to these body postures was found in the religious trance of an agricultural religion. It was through witnessing speaking in tongues in a fundamentalist Christian church that Dr. Goodman rediscovered the postures as a lost tradition. The body postures as ritual had been lost, but the last threads of ecstatic trance remained—and that was enough.

The last chapter in the development of culture was the appearance of the city dweller. Today, as a culture, city dwellers are divorced from their habitat and dependent on agriculture for their food. Machinery and technology are designed to control the natural world, using everything from heat pumps for climate control, to Nautilus and Stairmasters for keeping bodies in shape, to the miracles of telephones and computers for communication. Just as the natural world is now more distant, so is the spirit world. For hunter gatherers and horticulturalists, contact with the Alternate Reality resulted in a gift or power, such as a story or the ability to heal. In agricultural religions, including those of today, contact with the spirit world comes in the form of receiving grace. For city dwellers, contacting the spirit world is more an indirect experience, accomplished perhaps through movies or computer games. Alternate Reality is more easily perceived as "outer space," and the beings who inhabit that space are identified as aliens. It is no surprise that city dwellers are beginning to hunger for a return to an ecologically balanced world and for spiritual experiences that belong to their own bodies.

When Dr. Goodman began her research in 1977, she could not have guessed where it would lead. Her work unveiled a simple secret: the human body with its central and peripheral nervous systems, is a great common denominator for the peoples of the world. By aligning and adjusting our bodies in very specific ways, we can consciously enter the wonderful and mysterious realm of spirit known to the spiritual traditions of all humans, known variously as the Dreamtime, the Garden, the Sky World, and Heaven.

In the years since 1977, nearly fifty postures have been gleaned from ethnography books, museum exhibits, newspaper articles, and even postage stamps. It seems fitting, however, that the oldest posture was unearthed by archaeologists close to Dr. Goodman's Hungarian homeland, in the Danube River valley near Krems. The figure of a woman chipped from a piece of slate had been broken into nine small pieces that were fitted together by Christine Neugebauer, the archaeologist who directed the dig. The figure's upraised arm and the peculiar twist of her right leg were cues that this might be a ritual body posture. Dr. Goodman first saw a picture of the little figure in an anthropology publication in Europe; then a group of us in Columbus participated in the first experimental trance with it in 1989. Later, groups in Europe substantiated what we learned—that it provides the most powerful and multidimensional journey into the realm of spirits of any of the known postures. This little Venus of Galgenberg, as she is now named, is 32,000 years old.

It was sobering to realize, as we stood in a circle with our left arms raised and our right feet angled just like this Venus stood, that we were continuing a practice that has been part of the human experience for 32,000 years. Because we had no human teachers, we had to rely on experimental methods, on what had been written about the religious traditions of horticulturalists and hunter gatherers, and on the benevolence of those in the spirit realms to guide us. We did not know how the women from Galgenberg entered trance 32,000 years ago, but from our own experience we knew that they understood that a ritual posture would guide their way into Alternate Reality. Using the same posture, we also journeyed to the realms where the first order of all things exists. There, the spirits taught us what we needed to know.

Those of us who teach workshops are regularly asked how we determine the specific uses of a posture. How do we know that the Chiltan Spirits are called upon for healing and the Tennessee Diviner for answering questions, especially about ritual? Determining the uses of the postures has been a process that has unfolded over time. At first, the process relied entirely on Dr. Goodman's perceptiveness, intuition, and knowledge of the ethnographic literature; now there are others who have the experience and knowledge to contribute to the learning.

The clues come primarily from the trances of those who experiment with unknown postures. In the earliest research, Dr. Goodman reported on her findings about the Nupe Mallam, which is now accepted as a divining posture: "One of the yoga teachers reported seeing the top of a church steeple: 'It spins and then bursts. I am everywhere and know everything.' And the second one said, 'I am piercing a veil and can gain understanding.'. . . For one, the light spiraled, and she felt pushed away by it. 'I understood,' she said, without being able to say what."[13] Divination has been defined by scholars Lessa and Vogt[14] as the art or practice of foreseeing future events or discovering hidden knowledge through supernatural means. It is not hard to recognize embryonic divination in the reports of these neophytes, who described "knowing everything," "piercing a veil and gaining understanding," or who said simply "I understood." When the reports of many, many women and men are slowly and carefully reviewed and compared, the purpose of each posture is revealed. Sometimes the interpretation starts off on the wrong track, but with time and experience, the uses of a posture become clear.

As a psychologist, I ask how we can discern the difference between our own projections and the clear perceptions of Alternate Reality. Of course, all perceptions, whether in this world or in nonordinary reality, are subjective. Modern physics continues to provide evidence that nothing is truly objective because the viewer has an effect on what is being viewed. So we must not accept only one person's view of reality. If we believe we know what type of experience a new posture mediates, then we can go back into trance and ask if this hunch is true. Each round of questioning further refines our understanding. As there develops a stronger community of individuals who are on more intimate terms with the ritual body postures, these individuals are better able to rely on each other to get an overview of the use of a new posture.

I often refer to the Hindu fable "The Blind Men and the Elephant." A group of blind men came upon an elephant and wondered what on earth it was. Each had his own perspective. The one touching the trunk pronounced that the elephant was like a serpent, while the one at the tail proclaimed that it was like a rope. Another wrapped his arms around a leg and decided the elephant was like a tree, and yet another found a huge flapping ear and was sure the elephant was like a fan. The moral of the story is obvious. Limited to our own individual perceptions, we can draw erroneous conclusions, but our collective experiences, drawn together, reveal a larger picture than any one of us can see alone.

It is very important as we share our experiences in trance that we do not fall into a trap of analyzing the images as though they were not real experiences. They are real occurrences in a reality separate from, but related to, the reality that we know as our ordinary lives. Our unique characteristics—our physiological traits, emotional makeup, cognitive style, and spiritual orientation—all affect what we are able to perceive in that other reality, but our experiences are not the products of our imaginations or totally a reflection of the personal unconscious. While the personal unconscious may determine the lens through which we look, the scene itself exists separate from us. We may interact with it, but we do not create it.

Students of Jungian psychology often approach trance experiences as symbolic events. However, these experiences are not symbolic in the linguistic sense, by which symbols are viewed as "mere markers of communications about abstract matters."[15] These are not abstract events, but perceptions of a reality that we see, smell, taste, touch, and hear. Trance experiences sometimes fit the definition of "symbolic" in the metaphorical sense, however. In them, we may see what is most meaningful to us individually, in the same way that dreams are clothed in symbols that evoke very specific associations based on our personal life experiences. Another example of this concept of metaphorical symbolism in trance is a tradition among the Pueblo Indians. It is understood by the Pueblo people that humans cannot look directly on the face of a spirit and live, so the spirits wear masks that allow humans to safely look at them. They are known to wear masks by which their human friends can most easily recognize them.

In one of my earliest trance experiences, I was greeted by Mickey and Minnie Mouse, Goofy, Pluto, and a whole trainload of other Disney characters. I had done a divining posture, asking in quite a serious way for information about a counseling center I was trying to create. I had seen each possible location symbolically in trance: one became a cathedral, and another became the Neuschwanstein castle that crazy King Ludwig II had built. My ideas for the center were clearly too big and grandiose. The office where I was then working appeared as a scene from Snow White in which the Seven Dwarfs went through the front door singing, "Hi ho, hi ho, it's off to work we go." As I followed them, the doorway became a tunnel. When we emerged from the other end of the tunnel, which provided the transformative experience, we were all on a train accompanied by Mickey and Minnie and the others. The spirits were not above donning masks from my culture to help me understand the answer to my question. I associated the Disney crew with a group of beings who suffered all kinds of hair-raising adventures and always survived with an attitude of lightheartedness. It was good advice, which ten years later still works for me and for my partners in the counseling center we established the year following this trance.

I have been doing dreamwork for about twenty years, dealing with my own dreams as well as those of friends and clients in my practice as a psychologist. The techniques of dreamwork are tools well suited to the understanding of trance experiences. In the Jungian tradition, *amplification* is the term used for the technique of referring to the literature of mythology and ethnography for an understanding of the unknown elements of a dream or fairy tale, or in our case a trance. The anthropologists who are part of the Cuyamungue Institute, and particularly Dr. Goodman, have contributed greatly to the understanding of individual trances and the specialized uses of postures by recognizing stories or themes that appear in the traditions of various cultures.

An example of amplification is described by Dr. Goodman in *Where the Spirits Ride the Wind.* She had a waking dream just before a small group of us arrived at her house to try the Chiltan Spirits posture for the first time:

A row of curiously shaped masks appeared before a background lightly blushing into rose. They were white and round, delicate like Chinese
paper lanterns, yet with their pointed ears they recalled the heads of cats.
The place for the eyes was cut out, and inside each one a dark-gray hairy ball
was incessantly in motion. Several times I was given to understand emphat-
ically that 'we lick blood, we lick blood.' . . . (T)hat same afternoon, I finally located the report that belonged with the photographs (of the posture).
. . . It seems that in Inner Asia, in the valleys of Uzbekistan, shamanesses ask
for the help of a group of spirits called Chiltan when they are called upon to
cure. The Chiltan are said to be forty-one young girl knights. . . . Their
favorite color is white, and in agreement with what I had been told in my
vision, the shamanesses smear the blood of sacrificial animals on their tambourines, because the Chiltan spirits like to lick blood.[16]

Along with amplification, personal association can also be used to
understand trances in the same way it is used to interpret dreams. In a
recent workshop, a group of fourteen of us did the Carchi Woman posture for the first time. Earlier in the day we had done the Adena Pipe posture, and as a group we had been told that the posture could be used to
ask a question about healing. We followed with the Carchi Woman posture to allow the healing to be accomplished. David, a psychotherapist,
shared this experience:

My legs were cracking open and vines growing out of them. The
vines were over my whole body. Then my body became a mass of incense,
the smoke moving out into the world. As more roots came out of my body,
they grew into the Earth, down into a place where there was an inner sky
and a lake of light with light coming up, up into the roots and vines. The
vines began to bear fruits. Some of the fruits opened and birds flew out,
and demons also. Suddenly I became a Buddha boy with my chakras lighting up with the light from the inner lake. People were coming up to me to

get the fruits and receive the light. I was able to sustain the hungry and help
to heal the people who were hurt. And I was laughing, a laughing Buddha
boy.

In his process of making personal associations to the elements in his
trance, David acknowledged a need to open up and release both the positive and the negative, both the birds and the demons. He was also clear
about needing to become more grounded, more rooted into the Earth as
his trance had told him. It was in the Earth that he would find the spiritual light to nourish not only himself, lighting up his chakras, but also
those who came to him for help and healing.

I asked David what he associated with the words "Buddha boy." He
grinned and said that the Buddha was fat and happy, an interesting counterpart to his own tall, skinny frame and serious demeanor. He agreed
that maybe the image of the Buddha boy was a reminder for him to laugh
and relax as he worked with his clients, something he did easily in other
situations. He was reminded that the Buddha boy was able to sustain the
hungry and heal the hurt, things that sometimes felt like overwhelming
tasks for him.

Questions arise about the extent to which we project our own cultural, psychosocial development, and psychological processes onto these
postures that come from indigenous, pre-agricultural societies. To some
extent, such projection is inevitable. In trance we expand beyond the limits of our cultural constraints to experience the Alternate Reality known to
early hunters and those who first planted gardens. But we never escape
being who we are. That is a spiritual lesson to be learned again and again,
and one that seems to be the message from many elders in native cultures.
We can learn from others, but in the end we must address ourselves and
our tasks as the people we are, living in a technological age on the brink
of disaster and transformation at the same time.

The worldview into which we are invited when we enter ecstatic trance is well described in Roberta and Peter Markman's overview of the spiritual world of Mesoamerica:

> In the shamanic world everything is alive, and all life is part of one mysterious unity by virtue of its derivation from the spiritual source of life—the life force. Because matter and spirit are separate yet joined, and material realities are the results of spiritual causes, to change material reality, the spiritual causes had to be found and addressed through ritual and visionary activity that enabled the shaman as mediator to move between the visible and the unseen worlds, thus linking the natural with the supernatural and life with death. This shamanistically conceived world was, therefore, not a world of animals and plants, of killing and harvesting so that they might survive, but a world of the spirit made manifest in these material things that surrounded their material bodies.[17]

The ritual postures allow us to reach into our collective past to bring into consciousness this wisdom that is part of our human heritage and to integrate it with our present knowledge and understanding. The good news in the midst of our current global crisis is that cultural change continues to take place. When the source of that change is an eternal wellspring in the Alternate Reality, there is the promise of a positive flow through the cycle of diversification and integration. The ritual postures bring us the means for returning to that wellspring. Using the postures, we can experience an underlying structure of reality. The postures are like codes or algebraic formulae that hold the meanings of specific structures existing timelessly in Alternate Reality. At the most abstract levels, these structures are ultimate and unchangeable. However, there is a level at which the structures are more flexible and changeable, fluctuating according to the unfolding of the universe and all of life within it. As we use the postures, we gain access to the archetypal stories in Alternate Reality and uncover the formulae. At the level of the fluctuating structures, new myths are emerging based on changes taking place in the biography of Planet Earth.

I had my own instruction in the importance of being an active participant in that recurring dance of change. The lesson was taught me early in my introduction to ecstatic trance, the second time I used the posture of the great Bear Spirit. I was at the Cuyamungue Institute and frankly was overwhelmed by the altitude, by the fact that I was the only native English-speaking person in the group of nine, and by the neurological overload of three trances a day (we had not yet learned that two a day is an appropriate limit for a workshop). After an initial struggle to shift into the trance state, I felt a large grizzly place his giant paws and sharp claws on my shoulders. His grip on me hurt, and I told him I could not continue with that much pain. The bear said he understood pain and had suffered much himself, but he did not let go. Then there appeared, in sequence, three men, all Native Americans, who later became my guides and teachers. I was in awe of them and humbled by their presence. I asked them why they bothered to come to me, and they made it clear that while I learned from them, they also benefited from our interaction. From them I understood that spirits, no matter how great or wise, require the help of those of us who have material bodies. Consciousness cannot be made manifest in the physical world without the help of those of us who live here. We always have our part to play in bringing spirit into matter.

In order to be practitioners as well as explorers in the complex realms of Alternate Reality, we need to learn more than the signature experiences associated with specific postures. There is an entire system of rituals that span the activities and spiritual needs of humans throughout a lifetime. There are postures that teach us about the transitions of birth and death, others by which we can ask divination questions, yet others for healing, and some for celebration. As we become familiar with these realms, we learn not only which postures are best used for certain purposes but also the specialized uses of each posture within a category. For example, if there is a question concerning a healing, then we consult the spirits using the Adena Pipe posture. If the healing task is a strenuous one, we know to draw upon the combined energies of the forty-one girl knights who are the Chiltan Spirits. For metamorphosis of what is imbalanced, we use the Carchi Woman posture. When there is dross or stale energy to be released, we call upon Tlazolteotl, the Aztec goddess known as the "eater of impurities."

Nearly fifty ritual postures have been identified, and more are being discovered. Those of us who have been researching the postures with Dr. Goodman do not anticipate that the collection of ritual trance postures will be endless, but we do believe that this first round of discovery will soon be concluded. In this round we have learned, first of all, how to identify postures. We know that some, like the Bear Spirit posture, are found around the world and have existed across centuries of time. Others, like the Carchi Woman and the Lady of Thessaly postures, have shown up in only one location. A few postures exist as variants in different locations. For example, the Bahia posture from Ecuador resembles the Olmec Prince posture from the Gulf plains of Mexico, and both are metamorphosis postures. Similarly, the La Tolita posture is like the Chalchihuitlique posture, with a small but important difference in the left arm and hand.

Once our group at the Cuyamungue Institute learned to identify postures and discern their uses, we created a rough idea of categories. These categories define patterns among the postures, identifying them as useful for the same purposes. The categories define the range of human activities, the rituals that define our lives. Now, through the stories we experience in trance, we are learning about the multidimensional matrix that underlies our existence on this planet. The next layer of research and practice will be to use and teach the wisdom that has been made available to us at this emergent time on our planet to heal ourselves and the Earth. In so doing we may also be able to exchange information with the spirits and with the fluid aspect of the matrix. By living in partnership with the beings of Alternate Reality, there is hope that our world can become whole and healthy once again.

In one of our workshops a few years ago, Dr. Norma Leclair, a psychotherapist who has been actively involved with ecstatic trance for nearly ten years, had a vision: "There was a tree with deep gouges in its trunk from which grew many beautiful flowers, and there was an inscription: From the wounding a garden will grow." Black Elk, the Lakota medicine man whose great vision was shared with us by John Neihardt,[18] saw a sacred hoop made of the hoops of all nations, joined together, and in the center of the great hoop was an immense flowering tree that sheltered all the beings of the Earth. Is it too much to hope that the time has finally come for the Tree of the World to once again blossom and thrive?

The Practice of Ecstatic Trance

This handbook is intended to be an introduction to the ritual body postures and a guide for those who decide to undertake the journey into Alternate Reality using these postures. A more complete story of the initial discovery of the postures and the ensuing research into their usage is told by Dr. Goodman in *Where the Spirits Ride the Wind.* This book, along with two later notebooks, *Jewels On The Path,* Volumes I and II, is recommended reading for serious students of ecstatic trance.

Any book or handbook cannot, of course, replace direct experience. If you undertake the practice of ecstatic trance, you are encouraged to participate in workshops, both for the value of working with a trained facilitator and for the added benefit of the group's combined focus. A well-trained teacher offers instruction in the correct positioning of your body in each posture, facilitates the deepening of your trance through the structure of ritual and the commanding presence of rattle or drumbeat, and assists in the interpretation and amplification of what you see and experience in trance. Just as valuable in a workshop is the presence of fellow travelers in the varied realms of Alternate Reality. Individuals who have worked on their own or in small groups regularly comment on the increased potency of ecstatic trance experienced in a group of twenty or more. It seems that there is a cumulative effect, each person adding support and intensity to the group's visions. Given that these postures were originally used within the religious practices of tribes and small communities, it is not surprising that their effectiveness is enhanced in the context of interrelatedness.

To begin your work with the ritual body postures introduced in this book, I recommend that you select about five postures that seem appealing to you, perhaps because you are drawn to the images of the artifacts or the areas where they were originally found. Avoid paying too much attention to the meanings of the postures or the experiences of others who have used them. Just practice holding the poses by reading the descriptions and studying the illustrations. Then allow the wisdom of your body to guide you in finding the right positions. Once you experience the poses yourself, refer to the stories included in each chapter. When you approach the postures this way, the visions or sensations you experience are really your own, not the products of suggestion or imagination. Then you can begin to explore specific content areas to learn more about the characteristic applications of each posture.

The ritual postures are grouped in this book into seven categories: healing, divination, metamorphosis, spirit journeys, initiation, living myths, and celebration. The introduction to each category defines its organizing concept and explores its relevance within the range of activities fundamental to human spiritual life. Also included in the introduction is an overview of all the postures within that category, with suggestions about the particular issues that are best addressed by each posture. Prior to beginning the ritual of a trance posture, it is useful to consider your desire or intent for entering Alternate Reality. You can then decide which category best addresses your intent. By reviewing all the postures in that category, you can select the one that seems best suited for the purpose of the moment.

To use the ritual body postures on your own, it is helpful to follow a few simple suggestions to enhance their effectiveness. First, select a location that can be made into a sacred space, at least for the duration of the trance. It must be a quiet space and not subject to intrusion. Having sacred objects in the room, like crystals, feathers, rocks, or a medicine wheel, contributes to the sensation of entering a special place for a special purpose.

Second, do not eat during the hour or two preceding the trance.

Fasting is an ancient and well-respected tool for aiding the body's transition into an altered state of consciousness. At least avoid eating meat or any food that is difficult to digest on the day you undertake ecstatic trance.

In preparation for the trance, select a posture and take a few minutes to practice it so that your body feels comfortable in the position—or as comfortable as possible, since a few of the postures can be physically challenging. If you are using a tape of drumming or rattling, make sure that the tape player is ready to go and the volume is appropriate. Turn off the telephone, lock the door, and make whatever other arrangements are necessary to assure that you will not be disturbed during the trance.

Whenever possible, smudge the space and yourself with the smoke of an herb. Sage is traditionally used for cleansing in preparation for a ritual, although any naturally grown and dried herb is acceptable, especially if it is aromatic and indigenous to the area where you live. Smudge sticks, usually a combination of sage, juniper, and/or sweetgrass, are available in many stores that sell Native American or New Age books. Over a large flat shell (with a flat rock in the bottom to keep the shell from burning) or a fire-resistant bowl, light the herbs and then blow out the flames; allow the dried leaves to smoulder and smoke. Then use a feather or your hands to wave the smoke over your face, throat, and heart to cleanse the energy fields around your body. At the conclusion of your smudging, be sure to thank the plant whose body made the cleansing possible.

Next, make an offering to the drum, rattle, or other instrument with which you are inviting the spirits to be part of your ritual. In the group I work with, we usually offer some blue cornmeal to the spirit of the instrument. In the worldview of the peoples who introduced the practice of ecstatic trance, all things in this world have counterparts in the spirit world. The rattle or drum you are using has a spirit that can be awakened and, if called upon, must be "fed." Our group usually uses cornmeal to feed the spirit of the drum or rattle because corn is a sacred gift from the beings who live in the spirit world. According to legend, when the people were starving, the corn maidens came to them from the other reality and provided corn by splitting open their thighs. They gave their bodies so that the people would have food and could survive. To give blue cornmeal back to the spirits is a way of saying, "Thank you for your gifts." I have learned to breathe softly on the cornmeal first, as a way of saying, "This comes from me, Belinda; this is my breath so that you can recognize that it comes from me." Then I offer the pinch of cornmeal, first to the six directions—counterclockwise east, north, west, south, then above and below—then to the rattle or drum itself. With a small breath, I blow the cornmeal gently into the surrounding air, where the spirit of the drum or rattle can "eat" it.

Sometimes workshop participants question making the offering to the four directions in a counterclockwise direction. Each tradition has its own way. I move counterclockwise because it is said that everything in the spirit world is the opposite or mirror image of everything in the world of ordinary reality. As I begin the ritual for entering Alternate Reality, I acknowledge this other world by reversing the directions. One way is not more correct than another, but you should be consistent with whatever way you choose.

After you feed your drum or rattle, greet and invite all the spirits known to you to participate in your ritual and trance. Do this by drumming or rattling four times in each of the six directions. Then offer cornmeal again, after having breathed on it gently, to feed those spirits who have responded to your invitation. With a wave of your arm, release the pinch of cornmeal into the air, knowing that the spirits gather its essence as it falls to the ground.

Next, perform a simple concentration exercise to help calm and focus your mind. Sit comfortably. Focus on your breath as it enters through your nose and then, without effort, gently release it. There is no need to do any unusually deep or forceful breathing—just a series of even inhalations and exhalations. Each full breath counts as one; do fifty breaths, counting ten breaths on each finger of one hand. Now you are ready to turn on the tape, if you are using one, and assume the posture. If you are in a group, have everyone move into the posture and then begin the rattling or drumming.

The auditory stimulation of the rattle or drum induces the altered state of consciousness. Use an even, rhythmic sound of 200 to 210 beats per minute for a duration of fifteen minutes. (Audio tapes of rattling and drumming that sustain this rhythm are available from the Cuyamungue Institute; see appendix.) Live sound has rich reverberations that electronic equipment cannot yet duplicate. Nevertheless, experienced trancers say they rarely notice the difference between "live" rattling and a tape because the sound often sinks into the background very early in the trance. If you have difficulty keeping your concentration during the trance, bring the focus of your attention back to the sound. Following the rattle or drum restores your focus and leads your body back into an altered state of consciousness.

During the fifteen minutes of drumming or rattling, your only tasks are to remain in the correct position and to stay aware of what you are experiencing. Trance is not always the same. You may feel a change in your body temperature, find yourself rocking or swaying, or experience energy flowing through parts of your body. You may see patterns of color or witness complex visions that resemble watching a movie. Sometimes you may hear sounds or voices; if you find yourself interacting with an animal or other spirit, you may ask questions and receive answers. Occasionally, people even report smelling specific aromas.

In the early stages of learning ecstatic trance, it is common to question what is happening: "Am I in the right position?" "What am I supposed to be feeling?" "What if I am doing something wrong?" If you have thoughts like these during trance, encourage yourself to just relax and focus on the sound of the rattle or drum.

Once the rattling or drumming has stopped, move out of the posture and sit quietly for a few moments. Most people like to make a few notes about the experience to capture the richness of detail of the trance. Others prefer just to sit with the blissfulness or the profound effect of the trance. In workshops, you may sit in a circle and invite people to share what they have witnessed and experienced in the trance. It is remarkable to listen to the diversity but also the similarity among experiences. It is not unusual for people sitting together to share a landscape or be visited by the same spirit. This is, in fact, so common that if a newcomer is having trouble shifting into the trance state, you can seat this person between two more skilled trancers, to be taken along for the ride, so to speak.

On rare occasions, someone may have trouble coming out of the trance, often because he or she does not want to return to ordinary reality. In this case, it is helpful to have the person physically move out of the posture, to call his or her name quietly, and to offer a little water. If the person's blood sugar level has dropped, as it may in people who tend to be hypoglycemic, there may be complaints of mild dizziness or of feeling sick to the stomach. Any high carbohydrate food that is easily digestible, like fruit juice or a cracker, can be helpful. These problems are not common, but because they are possible, individuals who are just learning to enter the ecstatic trance state should use the postures in the company of others.

At the conclusion of the trance, you may wish to make a thin path of cornmeal from yourself or your circle to the nearest door or window. Traditionally this is the path the spirits follow to guide them away from the gathering, back to the freedom of their own existence. When you arrive at the open door or window, speak your gratitude to all those who came to help with the trance and then toss the remaining cornmeal into the air.

The ecstatic trance is not always what people expect, and sometimes there is doubt that anything at all occurs. However, there are several key indicators that confirm the altered state of consciousness. If you are concerned about having your concentration waver or are in doubt about being in trance, simply listen to the sound of the rattle. Once you are in trance, that sound tends to change. For some people the sound disappears. For many, the sound doubles, as if there are two rattles in the room, or it grows geometrically until the space is filled with the sound of rattles, which may become more like tinkling chimes or crickets or a waterfall. Sometimes the rhythm of the rattle changes or the volume grows louder or softer. Regularly, people in my workshops accuse me of altering the rhythm and volume, and I assure them that I have not done so. I know this, because maintaining a regular, even 210 beats per minute is crucial to inducing the trance, and those of us who are trained to give workshops have refined our ability to sustain this rhythm. Also, only a few people in the group usually hear the change in rhythm or volume, while the others do not. However, perceiving some change is one indication that you are in trance.

In the absence of any visual or auditory perceptions, a third indicator of trance is the occurrence of involuntary movements. Especially in the standing postures, you may find yourself twitching or swaying, bobbing your head, or grimacing, all involuntarily. I often begin introductory workshops with the Singing Shaman posture, a standing position and one of the few in which a sound is made. It is an odd but confirming experience to listen as the sound of your own voice changes, and to try unsuccessfully to control that sound. This, along with other body movements, helps you recognize the changes that are taking place, appropriately, in trance.

Postures are identified according to the names given them by Dr.

Goodman and the group of us who are colleagues at the Cuyamungue Institute. The postures were named according to one of several factors: the location where a figure was first discovered, like the Venus of Galgenberg; the name of the spirit being who is called upon in the trance, like the Lady of Cholula; the specific use of the trance, like the Psychopomp; or the nature of the experiences reported by early research subjects, like the Albatross.

Because of the similarities in the postures, it is important that you pay close attention to detail in assuming the physical position of a posture. When she was first researching the Chiltan Spirits posture in Europe, Dr. Goodman did not notice that some participants placed their left arms on top of their right arms, instead of their right arms above their left arms as shown in the photograph. Later, the reports of these few people were wildly different from the others. They told of experiencing dark, cold places, heavy with the presence of death, while most of the group saw the light and felt the boost of energy so typical of the presence of the young girl knights who are the Chiltan Spirits. Later, Dr. Goodman discovered that the arm placement is crucially important; with the left arm above the right, you take a spirit journey to the Realm of the Dead rather than experiencing healing with the Chiltan Spirits.

Once you have become familiar with contacting Alternate Reality, you may wonder whether it would be useful to incorporate ecstatic trance into your daily life. We have found that it is not helpful to use the postures on a daily basis. From observations of our own lives and from talking with workshop participants, it seems that the ritual body postures are most effective when they are coupled with another spiritual practice—like meditation, dreamwork, journaling, or a recovery program—that is performed each day. The postures are then used for special needs rather than for daily maintenance. Your daily spiritual practice becomes your tool for integrating the insight, wisdom, and healing that arise during the trance.

I do recommend meeting regularly with a group to try new postures, to deal with special needs of group members, or to just enjoy the experience of going to the spirit world together. Even experienced trancers usually prefer using the postures within a group. Sharing the journey to the spirit world creates a cohesiveness and helps you to develop the sense of community so often lacking in our culture.

Woven into the following chapters are accounts of participants in workshops and groups I have facilitated over the past ten years, along with stories that have been shared with me personally and in writing. These experiences are not a standard against which your journeys should be judged, but rather a sampling to introduce you to the possibilities available within each trance. The shamanic teachings that provide the foundation for ecstatic trance emphasize learning from your own experience. If your trance takes you into a different landscape than those described here, honor what you see, hear, and feel. There is no right way or wrong way, as long as you perform the postures accurately and with appropriate ritual and respect.

A written description accompanies a drawing for each of the ritual postures. The visual and verbal directions are intended to help you achieve the correct position. The important details are emphasized in the written description, and correct adherence to them is extremely important. Some aspects of the posture may vary among examples from around the world, and these variations are, in most cases, mentioned in the text. The descriptions focus on the subtleties of the posture that have been reinforced by its successful use over time.

Occasionally in trance, practitioners are instructed in minor body shifts that help determine how the posture is to be held. In these cases, the spirits are offering guidance since details of artifacts may be obscured. However, in their enthusiasm workshop participants have sometimes suggested trying variations of their own creation. This type of experimentation is discouraged because people usually feel discomfort and nausea when a pose is not a ritual body posture.

Through using these ritual body postures to achieve ecstatic trance, you are introduced into a different way of living on our planet. It is a way of life into which I have been adopted, just as my dream promised so many years ago. You are invited to join many others in this great adventure. In this greater reality, you may find hope and vision, a sense of meaning, and the longed-for feeling of coming home.

Welcome.

Healing

One of the primary purposes for entering Alternate Reality is to heal and be healed. In this context, healing has its original meaning: to make whole. In other words, healing means the restoration and maintenance of balance and wholeness. In the old days, medicine people had the identified task of continually restoring the disrupted balance of the natural world. There are stories from native people all over the world about problems that were caused when people did not live in right relationship with Mother Earth, all her creatures, and the beings who live in the spirit world. Maybe someone's body became diseased, or the tribe as a whole was affected—there was a drought or the game left and the tribe grew hungry without food. The healer's job was to discover the source of the problem and to bring back into balance that which had been disrupted.

Over time, the numbers of healers in the world have dwindled. In our modern urban world, we have a bevy of specialists to fix our brokenness. Physicians treat problems in the body, often from a narrow perspective of only one system in the body. Psychotherapists treat emotional problems. Ministers and rabbis and priests soothe troubled souls. Governments and agencies are designated to solve social problems. It is rare for all these specialists to consult each other to figure out how all the pieces fit back together.

In the old times, healers knew that problems were connected to every level of living. To make things right again, the help of beings who lived in the spirit realms was required. Much of the knowledge of indigenous healers has been lost, yet the work with posture-mediated trance indicates that every person can begin to fill, at least in small ways, the healer's role.

Judi's story offers an example of how ecstatic trance can be used for healing. Judi had a doctoral degree in agricultural economics and was teaching in a large midwestern university. Her work was dissatisfying to her, however, and over the course of several months, she realized that her real love was nature and the sense of magic and wonder she had felt as a child living close to the Earth. She longed for that connection again. She was also experiencing stiffness in her back and neck.

In the second trance she ever experienced, using a spirit journey posture, Judi "became a salamander and enjoyed the sensations of external gills, muscularity in my trunk and throat that facilitated catching and chewing dragonfly larvae (quite succulent!), and the extreme flexibility in the spinal column which was such a switch from my own stiffness and soreness that had been a constant for about six weeks." In other words, Judi underwent a brief metamorphosis into a salamander during her journey to the Lower World. Already, at this early stage of learning to use ecstatic trance, her connection with Alternate Reality was attuning her system to resonate with nonhuman beings and the condition of the world as they experienced it.

During the same weekend workshop, Norma, who was fairly sophisticated in posture-mediated trance, had a vision that she knew was for Judi. She told a story about the reflowering of a garden. Judi understood this story to mean that she could help restore part of the natural world that had been damaged. At the conclusion of the workshop, all participants joined in the Bear Spirit posture, for Grandfather Bear is the greatest healer in many societies around the world. In trance, Judi flew with an eagle over North America, landing in southeast Alaska. At the conclusion of her trance, she saw a flash of bright light, and a wave of heat poured through her body while a voice said, "You are a healer of the Earth."

Within the next three months, Judi was offered a job by the state of Alaska to work on the cleanup of the Exxon Valdez oil spill. Already her trance was becoming manifest in her life, for nothing could more clearly have been an opportunity to assist in the reclamation of the Earth. In preparing for her departure, Judi met with me to do a divining posture, the Nupe Mallam, to ask the spirits about the work she was to do in Alaska.

In that trance, Judi was instructed on a specific ritual that would hasten the healing of the oil-covered beaches. Included in her visions was an image of herself standing in an unfamiliar posture. She was puzzled by the stance and what meaning it might have for her. As I heard her description of the posture and began to visualize it, my eyes suddenly filled with tears. Judi was accurately describing a posture that had never been introduced in any workshop, that was not included in the handbook of ritual body postures published by the Cuyamungue Institute, and that she would not have known about prior to her trance. It was the Calling of the Animals posture, one of the few postures not taught by the Cuyamungue Institute because of its effect on living animals. It comes from hunter societies, and its purpose is to send out a beacon to the animal world, asking those who are willing to offer themselves for whatever purpose the person in trance has identified. It may have been used to call game, asking the animals to give of themselves so the people would have food. The context in Judi's vision was quite different, but the message seemed clear: Judi was to perform a ritual to heal the land and waters affected by the oil spill. Then she was to use the Calling of the Animals posture to invite the animals to return—to repopulate that which had been desecrated and would now be restored. This was Judi's chance to become a healer of the Earth, as the voice from the Bear Spirit trance had promised.

Judi's story is only one of many that describe the ways in which the spirits work with us. The religious specialists who originally practiced these postures did not create divisions between somatic, psychological, social, and spiritual problems. Hence, the ritual posture trances are useful for dealing with issues in any of these dimensions. Or, more accurately, the spirits who assist people in these trances respond to the multidimensional aspects of any presenting problem. Judi asked for help in finding a new direction in her career; she was not only given a way to help the Earth, but she also found relief from her neck and back problems during her metamorphosis into a salamander undulating through the mud.

Through trance it is possible to relieve pain and illness, or provide strength and hope for those whose disease at the physical level has progressed beyond recovery. Many practitioners have received suggestions for unorthodox treatments that are surprising but practical. Susan, for instance, had been diagnosed with condyloma and had had a class III reading on her most recent PAP test, indicating a precancerous condition of her cervix. She asked for help using the Chiltan Spirits posture and was told, in trance, to apply aloe vera directly to her cervix. Aloe is among almost everyone's collection of home remedies because of its reputation as the best medicine for small burns. It is good for healing skin tissue, and since the tissue of the cervix is made up of epithelial cells, the treatment made sense. However, just to be sure, Susan asked her gynecologist about this treatment; the physician was amused but agreed that it could help her and certainly would not hurt her. Over the next six months, Susan used the aloe vera. She also did more healing trances and sought the help of a psychic healer. At her next examination, her PAP test was normal. Her cervix has remained clear for the past three years. Would aloe vera help any woman with abnormal cervical cells? No one knows, but perhaps someone will investigate the potential in this remedy. It is a benign treatment for a condition that is affecting more and more women. At least for Susan, this remedy was a gift she gratefully received from Alternate Reality.

As a psychologist, I am also interested in using trance as a vehicle for emotional and spiritual healing. Diane's story offers an example of the use of a healing trance in counseling. Diane was concerned about her younger son, age fifteen, who was depressed and withdrawn. Although he had been in therapy for several years, he was not responding well. Diane recognized—through her dreams, meditations, and prior therapy—that subconsciously she and her son were closely connected. She was concerned that her own psychological issues were affecting him and wanted help in dealing consciously with her own dark side, hoping thereby to relieve him of any burdens he unwittingly carried for her. Together we decided to call upon Grandfather Bear, the old great healer.

As she went into trance, Diane saw a shaman kneeling on the ground, wearing a bear skin; the head of the bear was over his own head. He was spitting on the soil in front of him to make earth briquets that would burn steadily for a long time. This fuel was needed to keep alive a fire that was heating an enormous caldron of water. As she watched the shaman, Diane became aware that she always had a lot of "water" in her life in the form of deep feelings and intense emotions. She realized that she tended to overtax herself trying to keep everything cooking and boiling. She felt defeated when she was unable to remain "fired up" for long periods of time.

Diane's vision continued: "I saw myself standing with a huge Indian headdress from my head to my feet. I experienced several helpers brushing away the feathers from the interior of the headdress. The feathers were rotten and old and needed to be cleaned away. They completed their work and I was left standing with only the outer layers intact." As she explored her understanding of the feather headdress, she identified it as a manifestation of the biomagnetic, emotional, mental, and spiritual energy fields surrounding her physical body. The message to her was to clear out the old, rotten patterns of energy that surrounded her.

During my own trance with Diane, the panther mask I have hanging on the west wall of my medicine room suddenly moved to the south wall, facing Diane. The panther addressed her, asking, "What do you fear?" Then the Bear Spirit, whom I often see as a burly old grizzly, approached her. Sinking his claws into her rib cage, he opened her chest. Deep in her heart was an old-fashioned image of Jesus, like the picture on the paper fans my grandmother would bring home from church on hot summer Sundays. The Bear Spirit pulled Diane up by the shoulders and shook her like a rag doll. Once her body went limp, her spirit broke open and emerged moist and delicate, like a succulent, salmon-colored cactus blossom, to be cared for gently in its harsh desert landscape.

Diane talked with me about the rotten emotional energy she carried with her, especially her fears, as the panther suggested. She examined beliefs that had been deeply embedded in her heart from her early life as a nun. The Bear Spirit had loosened her up and showed her that inwardly she was delicate, which was a condition of beauty to be enjoyed rather than a deficit against which to defend. At the conclusion of our session, I suggested that within a few days she follow up with a spirit journey to the Lower World to ask an animal spirit to befriend her as she incorporated the wisdom and advice she had just received.

To create a ritual for healing, it is common to first use a divining posture to ask the spirits for guidance. Because each posture is a complete ritual in itself, this initial consultation may be all that is needed. In other situations, however, a more elaborate combination of postures and ritual elements may be called for. If the people involved are accustomed to trance on a regular basis, several postures may be used together.

For example, one afternoon a group of five people, including myself, gathered in anticipation of a healing ritual. We began by sharing with each other around the circle to clarify both the obvious and subtle issues of imbalance in our lives. Then we did a series of postures. First was the Tennessee Diviner posture, in which we asked for guidance regarding the elements needed in the healing ritual. Then we did the Adena Pipe posture to ask for very specific information about what needed to be healed in each of us individually as well as within the collective we represented. This was followed by a ritual given to us by the Tennessee Diviner in the first trance. Three of us formed a triangle, each in the Singing Shaman posture, and directed energy toward the other two while they went into the initiation trance of the Greek Youth and Maiden posture.

Certainly it was a strenuous afternoon. A series of three fifteen-minute trances requires being in shape, and I do not recommend an extended ritual such as this one to a beginner. It would be like suggesting that an inexperienced climber hike to the top of Yosemite's Half-Dome. Nevertheless, for those who are prepared for it, it is potent work, opening up the possibility of a sequence of postures directed toward a specific goal.

As you consider using healing trances not only for yourself but to become a healer in the world, a few issues warrant consideration. Those who have earned the right to be called healers have committed their lives to healing and have often endured severe initiations. While you are learning, it is very important that you respect your limits and not attempt to go beyond what you are able to do. That is not easy advice to follow. Some people are very cautious and do not want to rise to challenges if presented with difficult but manageable situations. Others are overly self-confident, underestimating problems and then getting in over their heads. Usually, if you are honest with yourself, you know what your tendencies are. If you are cautious, ask for help and support and take a few risks. If you know that you are prone to believe you can handle anything, slow down and ask for guidance in understanding the full implications of the issue you are offering to help heal.

As a psychotherapist, I am well aware of the blind spots people have in their psyches. Adequate training for all counselors requires that some attention be given to identifying these blind spots so that their own issues are not projected onto those they would help. One of the biggest problems I witness among healers and helpers is ego investment in helping and curing. To be genuinely successful in your work, you have to know that you work in cooperation with many forces, and your task is only to do your part, then let go.

A final caution is a reminder of the old shamanic traditions in which healers were required take on the diseases of their patients. The healers' task was to heal themselves first and then to cure their patients by the same means. This is not the same as unconsciously absorbing the energy of the patients. Proper training for all therapists includes methods for disconnecting from clients' energy fields. However, in the context of shamanic healing, be well advised: Whatever you choose to heal, be sure you are willing to have it affect your life.

There are specialized uses for each of the healing postures. The Bear Spirit posture is very powerful and can be used for healing either yourself or others. My colleagues and I use it at the end of many introductory workshops to bring the group, and the individuals within it, into a new balance. Participants need this balance as they integrate their trance experiences into an expanded understanding of themselves and the world. The Chiltan Spirits posture and the Couple from Cernavoda posture each has a distinctive version for men and for women. The male version of the posture allows the man to serve as a battery, channeling supportive energy to the woman, who accomplishes the healing task. These two postures are especially useful for healing others and are recommended when the "patient" cannot be physically present. The Carchi Woman posture deals with the origins of imbalance in the body, offering through metamorphic changes the possibility for a new or renewed form to emerge. The Empowerment posture is included among the healing trances because it draws empowering energy into the person in trance. When you are depleted by illness or stress, this is a posture for restoring an abundance of your life force. Tlazolteotl is an Aztec goddess known to eat impurities. When you do her posture, she offers to consume the physical and emotional dross you are releasing in order to be well, and in so doing assists you in your healing.

THE BEAR SPIRIT POSTURE

The name of this posture is derived from a wonderful carving of the Northwest Pacific Coast Indians in which the Grandfather Bear Spirit, the Great Healer, stands behind a shaman who holds the pose. It is very old and, of all the postures, is the most widely known. Evidence of it has been found in countries throughout the world, and historically it has existed from 6000 B.C. to the present. In Egypt and Mesoamerica, this posture even survived the shift from horticulture to agriculture. *Where the Spirits*

Ride the Wind[19] contains a global map showing the variety of locations where the Bear Spirit posture has been found.

The task of the Great Healer is not just to cure disease but to restore harmony and balance. With balance and harmony intact, the health and well-being of the individual and community are maintained. Images of this posture are found so frequently that it has likely been used in many societies as an ideogram to convey the message "Good health to you!"

The Bear Spirit is known to many as Grandfather Bear, with all the affection and respect this name connotes. People in workshops who do this posture for the first time often experience Grandfather Bear's deep love and feel a profound sense of joy. One of the youngest trancers I worked with, a twelve-year-old boy, told me he kept feeling like he was falling backward during this trance, but someone was always there to catch him. He was going through a difficult time emotionally—dealing with a father whom he loved very much but who was at times physically and emotionally abusive. Having the Bear Spirit behind him to catch him when he fell gave this boy a sense of security that he badly needed.

At difficult periods in my life, I have come to Grandfather Bear for help and he has unzipped the front of his big shaggy body and invited me to sit inside him. There, completely surrounded by his massive being, I have felt him absorb all the emotional and physical toxins within me. This experience has been repeated enough times that I now feel myself able to absorb some of his strength. It is not unusual for others in this trance to have some experience of being split open. Then they receive a flow of energy or a specific substance—one woman called it royal jelly, like the substance produced by bees—from outside themselves. Many people describe having their bodies scored by the Bear Spirit's claws to release impurities as part of a healing ritual within the trance. And even though being torn apart or dismembered is a frequent theme in this posture, rarely do people report the suffering that is so often experienced by Siberian shamans as their bodies are torn apart in trance.

Susan experienced such a healing trance with Grandfather Bear:

> I start crying immediately. I see myself entering a large round build-
> ing made of saplings and covered with a brown, feltlike cloth or skins. The
> floor is a very lightly packed dirt floor. I walk, am led to the center, where
> briefly my chest muscles are pierced as for a Sundance. I have no breasts.
> The physical pain is a welcome relief from the emotional pain contained
> within my body.
>
> There is a circle of bears. One comes up to me and tears my head off,
> and the crunching sound of my vertebrae is also a welcome relief to the pres-
> sure contained there. I see the big, tall brown bear as he comes up to me,
> and I am flooded with emotion, crying out loud. Inwardly I say to him,
> "Grandfather, heal me, restore me to balance, I am in pain." Bears gather
> around me and score my back and upper arms and thighs with a pattern
> similar to Joanne's. Then they take claws and open muscle-ropes in my
> neck—there are round white things, like snow peas, that keep popping and
> spilling out. Then my legs, calves [are torn] lengthwise and blood spills out,
> and it feels good, like draining toxins from me. Then upper legs and some
> in torso. Along my spine, between each vertebra, is one of those round
> things, one on the left and one on the right of each vertebra. At the base of
> the spine is a white round heart, almost glowing. I don't know what that is
> or what it means. Bear makes an opening at the top of my head, and a
> knobby white growth protrudes from it. Later a similar opening is made in
> my brow. Pouring some fluid down my spine to replenish the loss of blood.
> [Be]came conscious in the center of the yurt again and the bears are danc-
> ing in a circle around me. They say and sing that they love me and welcome
> me into their midst. I cry again, this time with relief at feeling so loved and
> welcomed. I felt new.

Even though Susan's ordeal was painful in one sense, she did not suffer. People rarely report having real physical pain during this trance.

Once, however, MaryAnna asked for the healing of six different people and the Earth, all in one trance. Even though this is one of the most simple postures to execute physically, she was in great physical pain throughout the experience. I believe that we sometimes suffer for those we are healing, and MaryAnna probably took on too much for one fifteen-minute session.

It is common for people to physically move in this posture—to sway, bounce, rock, shake, or dance. They may jerk around like rag dolls, shake, be pushed, or otherwise lose their balance. No one has ever fallen during this standing trance, however. Along with these movements, people frequently get hot. The intense heat is associated with being healed.

Judy reported on one experience with Grandfather Bear:

> I stood facing a huge fire. I was dancing, or more like stomping my feet up and down to the rhythm of the drum. It was like dancing in place. Bear said I needed to sweat. I did, a lot! Then I was in a domed grass hut and was rubbed down with sage. I could smell the sage. I started to sway, and that made me want to throw up or scream. The scream seemed like a huge roar in my throat that needed to release something. My palms were very sweaty. I was exhausted after the posture.

Trancing sometimes requires huge amounts of energy. Especially after a healing, it is important not to strain your body or nervous system while the healing "takes." After the trance, rest, drink a lot of water, and get plenty of sleep. Any kind of focused or intense activity is not a good idea for the rest of the day.

However, the process of healing is not always so strenuous. People who perform the Bear Spirit posture often report on the healing effects of nature's beauty. Beth came to the Bear Spirit for help in dealing with a series of losses in her life. In trance, she saw herself standing on the edge of a mesa, watching a beautiful sunset; there, she was at peace. Sometimes

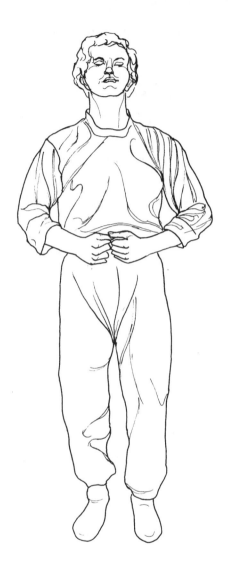

a healing comes in the form of words of wisdom and advice, such as "See things as they are, not as you want them to be," or "Our healing is to become one with our opposite."

At times, instead of seeing the Bear Spirit, people may see his helpers, such as the snake or the owl or carrion-eating birds. The color purple is characteristically part of this trance, and is sometimes seen instead of the Bear Spirit.

DESCRIPTION

Stand with your feet parallel, about six inches apart, and your toes aimed straight ahead. Your knees should be slightly bent, removing any strain on your lower back that would occur if your knees were locked. This stance is consistent for most of the standing postures. Gently roll both your hands, as though you are holding a small egg in the palm of each hand. Position your hands so that your folded fingers form a tall triangle over your navel. The first joint of the index finger of each hand should touch to form the apex of the triangle, with your thumbs resting one in front of the other, not one on top of the other. Your upper arms can rest easily at both sides of your body, so that your elbows are not sticking out. With your eyes closed, lean your head back as though you are looking at a point just above the line where the wall meets the ceiling. There may be a strained feeling in the muscles at the back of your neck.

A kneeling variant of this posture has been found only in the form of a woman. This kneeling position produces the same characteristic heat and experience of being opened up and filled. It is especially useful for relieving menstrual cramps. Instead of standing, kneel with your knees close together and your buttocks resting on your heels. The positioning of your hands and head are the same as in the standing version.

THE CARCHI WOMAN POSTURE

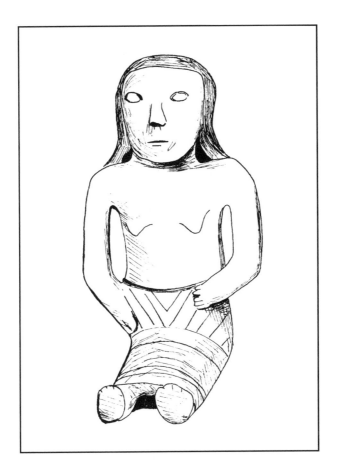

This posture was discovered recently in a beautiful book of photographs of Ecuadorian pottery figures published in Germany. Carchi, where this figure was found, is a mountainous province in northern Ecuador, bordering on Colombia. It is an area subject to frequent earthquakes; Tulcan, its major city, was severely damaged by one in 1923. The culture that produced this figure dates from A.D. 800 to 1500.

Many of the postures found in the book of Ecuadorian figures appear to be for the purpose of metamorphosis. However, in the trance experiences of workshop participants, this small woman characterized herself more as a healer, even though her style of healing is different from that of the Bear Spirit and Chiltan Spirits. Jan Price is a psychotherapist and, as one of the original members of the Columbus group, has worked with ritual body postures for over a decade. Jan describes the Carchi Woman posture as helping people to reach a deeper level of empathy or compassion. Healing occurs in the process of relinquishing whatever interferes with compassion. Indeed that is an accurate definition of metamorphosis: obtaining a profound level of empathy with another being. I believe that this posture allows healing to occur through a process of metamorphosis; the body is literally changed as it moves into syzygy with a form or pattern that is whole. Jan suggests that when you are healed in the Carchi Woman posture, it is possible for a change to take place in your DNA molecules, recreating some aspect of your body for all time. One workshop participant described the changes she experienced in this posture as cascades of energy going back to the Source.

When Judy asked the Carchi Woman for guidance about the purpose of this posture, she concluded from her trance that it "seemed to me a way of helping something emerge into form." This would account for how often people see wombs in this trance. Carol reported: "In the left field [of vision], I was at the opening to a womb and the inside spiraled—then an angel of light came from above and went into the womb." In my own first experience with the Carchi Woman posture, the full moon became a spotlight and shone on my uterus, lighting it up. Later I witnessed the change of form that describes the healing process, although not the experience of metamorphosis. I saw a bird that became smaller and smaller until it was only an embryo. Then I saw a broken egg; the yolk was gold and looked like a bubble of mercury. It became gold dust and disappeared. The mercury becoming gold and then disappearing was a clue to the transformation, this time in alchemical terms. Interestingly, two years later a woman said at the end of her trance, "I also saw an egg hatching and I knew that all society has to be born."

Many people performing this posture experience both light and darkness, whether in the form of a womb or a crypt or just plain darkness. The darkness and light go together. Pamela said, "I saw a landscape kind of dark with lavender and pink in the sky. There was a huge white rose, brilliant and glowing like the moon." Lavender, pink, and white are commonly reported with the Carchi Woman. The movement from darkness to light suggests the changes taking place. MaryAnna reported: "I saw the face of a baby seal very close to my face. . . . Its eyes became very dark, then 'receded,' and when it came up close again it was very bright and became a star, then back to an eye—this time of a bird—then bright and became a flower."

The heat of this healing posture may not be as intense as it is in the Bear Spirit posture. Judy said she was "nice and warm, the kind of warmth that goes through you." Others, however, spoke of a tremendous amount of heat and fire.

Finally, people performing this posture repeatedly experience a beautiful woman. In one case, she was a huge white spider who changed into a white-haired woman. Another person described "the figure of a seated native woman, all white on a burgundy background, posed as a Gorman [the Navajo artist R.C. Gorman] woman would be." Yet another person described that feminine being as "the Eagle spirit [who] reached out with her long soft wing."

These various characteristic experiences were integrated in a trance report sent to me by Gwyn. She had asked the Carchi Woman for help in learning how to manifest love and healing in her life. She wrote:

> I saw a woman looking like the figure in the posture dancing around
> in a very playful way. Then she lifted me up on the back of a horse in front

of, even in the lap of, a Native American woman who was luminescently beautiful. I was taken on a journey into an opening, like a mouth of the Earth, and into the very core center of the Earth. This woman began to dig in the dark, fragrant soil in the center of the Earth and to plant seeds of all sizes and shapes. She said that each seed she planted was for a relationship. I got down and began to plant seeds with her, next to her.

The activity of healing with the Carchi Woman is very personal, and may not even seem to be related to your physical body. Nevertheless, you may feel yourself change inside, and your life experience validate the changes.

DESCRIPTION

Sit on the floor with your legs close together, extended straight ahead, with your knees locked. Your feet should be at right angles to your legs, so that the soles of your feet face forward. Hold your back erect, forming a right angle with your legs. You may need to lean against a wall or other prop, which will not interfere with the trance. Hold your left upper arm stiffly away from the body, with your left hand placed on your abdomen at waist level and the middle finger of your left hand pointing to your navel. Cup your right hand and place the ball of the hand at your waist. Point your right fingers, held closely together, toward the floor. Face forward, with your eyes closed.

THE CHILTAN SPIRITS POSTURE

Modern shamanesses in Uzbekistan, a state of the former Soviet Union located in central Asia, sit cross-legged in this posture. In their trances, they are said to summon the spirits of forty-one girl knights who assist them in their work of healing. In their healing ritual, these shamanesses smear tambourines with the blood of sacrificed animals as an

offering to the spirits in return for their assistance. The Chiltan Spirits, as the spirits of the girl knights are known, like to lick the blood.

This posture is named for these Chiltan Spirits, even though the same posture has been identified in a variety of other locations. In Bolivia, a statue in this posture was chiseled into a 3000-year-old stone column. A recent publication about antiquities of Tennessee included a picture of a stone sculpture in this position, dating from A.D. 700. And in Alaska's

Sitka National Monument there is a Haida totem pole, used as a corner post for the roof of a house, into which is carved a man in this posture.

In the Chiltan Spirits trances, there is always some manifestation of multiple energies that express the presence of the forty-one girl knights. Pamela, for instance, said, "[I saw] little light dots all around, and I was sitting in a teepee of pure light. The dots began to move and I felt like I was going downstream with them. They swirled and made a circle." People often see the image of a circle of women gathered around a fire in a cave. In one trance, I saw myself sitting with MaryAnna, Barbara, and others in a large, cool cave with a very high ceiling and a layering of fine dirt on the floor. This cave has become very familiar to me from doing this posture.

Because of all the energy available, this is a good posture for doing healing work for others, especially those at a distance. When I begin a healing session like this, I try to be rested and focus on the "patient," asking the Chiltan Spirits how I can be helpful. Once in trance, when I find the person for whom the healing is being sought, I ask if she or he wants to get better, and in more serious situations, if she or he wants to live. Following is an example of one such session taken from my notes:

> I found myself rocking S. on my lap. She said she was tired of living in this world, that it was too hard to live in a physical body with emotions, and she wanted to leave. I told her she could if she wanted to but she should be very sure about her decision. She said she felt relatives clinging to her. I told her that they loved her and would miss her very much, and that indeed they may be attached to her. Loving her helped them remember who they were, embodied spirits or souls who come to this plane but are not bound in it. Love is what helps us all remember who we really are. I talked with S. about who she would miss here, and told her that she had to be prepared to leave completely, that she couldn't change her mind after she left and attach herself to these people. We talked about going to the Sky World and

how we would do a posture for her [the Psychopomp posture]. I told her I would have to leave now, and she moved to her mother's lap, rocking while she decided whether she would leave or stay.

In this case, the real issue was this young woman's willingness to be alive. No other healing was relevant until she made her decision. She apparently did decide to live, and her condition began to improve soon afterward.

In a different situation, another woman was also uncertain whether she wanted to live, but she had enough willingness to allow her healing to proceed. I used the energy of the Chiltan Spirits in trance:

> I sliced her open and found her to be like an onion, with some layers brown and spoiled. We peel down the layers until we find a tiny little seed, like a mustard seed. I am reminded of the Biblical reference to faith being like a mustard seed, which is tiny but grows into a very large plant. I am told that the seed is very hard and needs to be moistened—with blood, semen, vaginal juices, spit, and tears. I sit over the tiny seed for days and days, chanting and watching over it. I am exhausted. Then a Native American woman comes, with long braids and dressed in white buckskin. I think she is a Corn Maiden. She takes the baby that has been born of the seed and holds it. I massage its tense little body. It is clear to me that the woman [the patient] is full of bitterness and resentment, and in the trance she becomes aware of it. She has to choose life instead of her bitterness.

Yet a third example was reported by Dr. Goodman in *Jewels on the Path* in the chapter entitled "The Gift of the Chiltan Spirits: A Healing in the City." Dorothy, a mutual friend who is a pediatric nurse, had called asking for help in dealing with a three-year-old boy for whom she was caring. He had been badly burned over most of his body, and there was some concern that he had also been sexually abused. Even though we were geographically separate, Dr. Goodman, Dorothy, and myself went into trance, asking the Chiltan Spirits for help in the healing of this little boy. Dr. Goodman wrote:

> It seems clear from our collective account that in a mysterious way we had been directed as a group to share the task at hand: it fell to me to alert the Chiltan Spirits; Dorothy funnelled their energy, which appeared in the multiple shape of the lions, toward the injured little boy; and Belinda carried out the healing itself. . . . As of May, Roger is out of intensive care. He is off medication and has no more seizures. His skin looks wonderful, it amazes everyone, there are no scars despite the fact that he actually did not have enough circulation to bring about that kind of healing.[20]

There are several techniques for healing that recur in the Chiltan Spirits trances of people who are experienced in this work. One is a process of slicing people open down the middle to reveal the location of the problem and to provide easy, "hands-on" access. Another is the use of sound and rhythm, like chanting over the patient, or hearing and using the sounds of the rattle to effect the healing. A third technique is the use of fire for purification. In one trance, Judy actually stepped into the fire at the center of the circle of women healers. This posture also continually invokes the presence of beautiful native women, such as the Corn Maiden in my experience. Others have called them "women in gauze," "women with huge diaphanous wings," or "[a beautiful woman,] tall with long straight hair and Mongolian features." Sometimes the woman is accompanied by a man. One person said about the man, "He had fingers of blue flame that touched me, perhaps burned me, but wonderfully, frighteningly so."

There is a love story associated with the Chiltan Spirits posture. Glimpses of it were revealed the very first time Dr. Goodman asked a small group of her colleagues to try this posture. The complete story was

discovered a year and a half later when Dr. Goodman was given a book about Alaskan totem poles. In *Where the Spirits Ride the Wind* she wrote:

> Looking for postures on those [totem] poles, to my surprise there was a Tlingit pole housed at Saxman Totem Park near Ketchikan, on which one of the carved figures, embraced from the back by a huge bear, stood in the Chiltan posture. When these poles were assembled and restored, the Forest Service asked the Indian craftsmen about legends they might know about the various poles. And for the pole in question . . . one of the artists recalled the legend about a man and a bear. It seems that a young man called Kats, who lived a very long time ago, when humans and animals were still as one, was caught by a grizzly bear. He was supposed to be eaten, but he was saved by the she-bear who fell in love with him and became his wife.[21]

Kats later was forced to return to his village through the magical intervention of one of his brothers because the village needed his skills as a great hunter. He moved to the edge of the village with his bear wife and cubs, trying to live in both worlds at the same time. His bear wife, who was a shamaness, warned him never to look at his former human wife, but he was trapped into seeing her. Upon learning of their encounter, his bear wife gave him a shove, and the cubs, seeing him no longer as their father but as a human man and therefore food, tore him apart.

How is this a love story? My first trance with the Chiltan Spirits was an enactment of the reunion of Kats with his bear wife. Dr. Goodman described me as "lending for a fleeting moment her human strength to the sorrowing spirit husband, and they [Kats and his bear wife] laugh as in the old days, when she found him so light, and they melt into each other in loving embrace." It was beautiful and poignant, this reunion of lovers after a timeless separation. Over the years, I have been invited during trance to share in the intimate details of the legend, which is much more than the love story just recounted. It has been a different sort of healing

experience for me, participating in the reunion of Kats and the she-bear through the vehicle of the Chiltan Spirits. Their story was a thread of hope during the grief of my divorce and also later, as I eventually found myself learning to love as the she-bear loved Kats. The layers and layers of meaning in the tale of Kats have been unexpectedly revealed to me by the Chiltan Spirits. And with each layer, my own heart has been healed.

DESCRIPTION

Female version: Sit in a cross-legged position, with your right leg crossed in front of your left leg. Place your left hand palm down against your waist, just to the right of your navel, so that your lower left arm extends along your waistline. Position your right hand palm down over your chest, with your lower right arm making a 30-degree angle from your lower left arm. Rest your upper arms against the sides of your body. Face straight ahead with your eyes closed.

Male version: *This posture is the same as the female version except that it is accomplished in a standing rather than a sitting position. Stand with your feet parallel, about six inches apart, your toes pointed straight ahead. Keep your knees slightly bent.*

THE COUPLE FROM CERNAVODA POSTURE

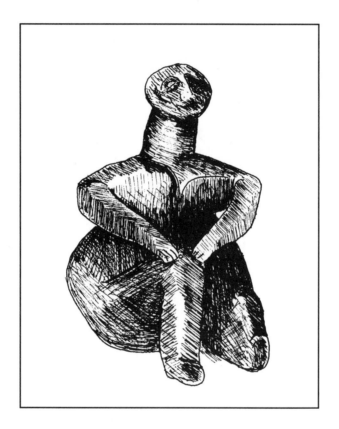

In a 7000-year-old grave near Cernavoda, in the Danube delta in Romania, a male figure in this posture was found alongside a female figure. Both figures were distinguished by stumpy feet, small heads on long necks, and black-brown coatings. Their similarities made it clear that they belonged together. The male figure was also discovered in other archaeological sites in Europe, dating from 5000 to 7000 years ago. Alone, he was called the "pensive god" or the "sorrowful god." Similar male sculptures were located in Africa, but the female figure rarely accompanied them.

Experiments with these two postures indicate that people in the male

posture act as energy sources for people in the female posture, who are the healers. When men work with women partners, they tend to have meager trance experiences, while the women report having powerful reservoirs of energy at their disposal to use in their shamanistic healing. When two women are partnered, one in the male posture and the other in the female posture, the same differences seem to occur.

MaryAnna, seated in the male version of the posture, with her friend

Kathleen in the female version, reported, "I seemed to be in a blackout of sorts, that is, no sound, no colors, no heat or cold. My field of vision was completely dark—nothing." Kathleen, on the other hand, began to breathe more deeply and in an exaggerated way. Vibrant colors folded in on themselves to create a kaleidoscope in her visual field:

> I recited the people's names and my horse's name that were needing a
> healing, several times. A figure appeared in front of me with a white, hood-
> ed robe on. Next I saw many arrows coming in from the right. I was told
> to see these going to each one of the people and the animal named. As I did
> this the arrows went straight for the heart [of each one needing healing] and
> exploded into tiny sparks of light.

The clear difference between the experiences of MaryAnna and Kathleen is an example of how partners function using the Couple from Cernavoda posture. While I have examples of women using the female posture alone for their own healing, two people working together are much more powerful.

One participant in a group of four noted a pattern of energy exchange among the four of them as they used the two versions of the posture. The two female healers donated their healing energy to each other and to each of the male "batteries," while the men exchanged "sparks" between themselves. The male support was absorbed and transmitted by the women.

The energy that flows through a woman healer in this posture is immense. One woman said she felt as though she had drunk a shot of alcohol: "It burned all the way down my throat and into my ribs." Another woman compared it to being a conductor for fire energy: "It came through me like waves of hot red/orange smoke and flames."

There is still so much to learn about how to direct this abundance of energy effectively. Kathleen's arrows, which directed the healing energy, have been seen by others. Judy, for instance, said she saw a crossbow that shot an arrow of light into her partner, who had kidney disease and who was seated across from her. The healer herself probably contributes a great deal through her calmness of mind and focus of intention. Following is an example from an experienced practitioner of ecstatic trance using this posture:

> I then saw a man. I don't know if it was Carol's brother. Carol had asked us to send some energy to him especially before the trance. Two people were shaking a rattle and drumming around him. The posture seemed very short to me. . . . The next day or so Carol mentioned to us that her brother got out of his hospital bed and walked for the first time in years. I don't know if Carol connected this with the posture work at all.

Of all the healing postures, this one is the least known. As more groups come together expressly to learn about healing, the Cuyamungue Institute intends to develop the healing abilities inherent in this ritual posture. It is the hope of those of us at the Institute that by focusing on particular diseases we may be able to discover ways of helping not only individuals but groups who are struggling with the same problems.

DESCRIPTION

Female version: *Sit on the floor with your left leg rigidly extended straight in front of your body. Keep your left foot perpendicular to your leg. Bend your right leg at the knee and, with your knee raised, place your right foot sole down on the floor, beside your left knee. Bend both your arms, with your elbows extending away from your body; bring together both hands and rest them lightly on your right knee. Hold your left hand stiff and arched backward, with the pads of your fingers resting on your knee. Keep your thumb close to your hand. Cup your right hand with your palm lifted and only your fingertips resting on your knee. Imagine yourself with a long straight*

neck like the unearthed figures, as a reminder to maintain a completely erect posture.

Male version: Sit on a low stool or on pillows piled on the floor. Place your feet on the floor in front of your body, pointing forward. Your feet are parallel and about eight to ten inches apart. Placing your elbows on your knees and, bending your arms, bring your hands toward your face until your head can lean forward slightly and be supported by your hands. Make a loose

fist with your hands. Allow the full weight of your head to be supported by your fists so that they push the skin upward making folds in the skin of your cheeks.

THE EMPOWERMENT POSTURE

    This posture was found in the form of a Mayan wood sculpture of a kneeling warrior or priest. The sculpture is unusual in that it had survived in the humid tropical lowlands of Central America where wood decays quickly. Additionally, it had been carved as a whole figure, rather than as part of a stela, which would have been more characteristic of the Maya. The stelae or carved panels told the stories of the Mayan people— stories about their daily lives and military victories, as well as their experiences in nonordinary reality. A figure similar to this one has been identified in modern Polynesia, and variations in a standing position have been attributed to the Minoan period of 2000 to 1700 B.C., and to the Persian of A.D. 100 to 300.

It seems appropriate that you could find your way to empowerment through the figure of one who appeared to be a Mayan priest prepared to engage in a ritual ball game well known from that culture. He wore on his hips the large protective yoke that enabled the players to hit the hard, heavy rubber ball. The ball had to pass through a ring, not much larger than the ball itself, that hung high on the side of the ball-court wall. The players were not permitted to touch the ball with their hands but had to use their hips and shoulders. The yoke, worn at the waist, was used to hit the ball. The game was more than a sport. In the Mayan myth told in the *Popol Vuh*[22], the hero twins had to play the ballgame with the Lords of Xibalba, the Underworld, as part of their initiation. At the conclusion of a ball game, one of the players was sacrificed; this was perhaps the beginning of the hero journey in the underworld modeled in the *Popul Vuh*.

Perhaps the priest in the wooden carving was preparing for a ball game, going into trance to garner the necessary physical strength for this unbelievably strenuous game. It is likely that he wanted to play well to honor the ritual of the ball game and to win. The sacrifice that was the culmination of the game fed the gods and thereby brought help to the people. From the perspective of this worldview, to discard the human flesh in order to return to the spiritual world was to give strength to the timeless cycle of life, death, and regeneration. One of my own early experiences in this posture enacted a portion of this life, death, and regeneration cycle. However, being from a culture that resists death, I was not initially able to honor it:

I saw a scene of mountains and a valley of pasture land, a man riding a horse, and the valley full of grazing buffalo. This scene was replayed several times, apparently in order to get it very clear. Then the rider became a Buffalo Bill character, and I witnessed the slaughter of the buffalo. Out of my mouth came an anguished cry— "No, no!" —and I wept physical tears. I felt like an Indian woman, crying in anger and dismay, asking the spirits how they could allow such a slaughter, allow such pain in the buffalo nation and the Indian nations. Slowly a voice came saying that we are only a small piece of a very large story. As that was repeated over and over again, my energy shifted to a kind of acceptance.

The message was that I had been trying to change patterns in the world that were not to be changed, and I could not be empowered to do so. The entire experience was exhausting rather than empowering, at emotional and physical levels. My legs were numb and my arms helplessly shaking by the time the trance was over. In rereading my notes, however, I realized that I had been directed toward practical matters— the tasks I could do, the changes I *could* effect. This was in no way a suggestion that the slaughter of the buffalo or the oppression of the Native American nations was right or justified in any way. It was, instead, a personal witnessing of the great cycles of life and death, and because I could not accept the death, I had not been able participate in the regeneration.

It is typical for people in this posture to experience flows of energy and to emerge from the trance feeling able to do anything. As one person described it, "Suddenly there was a surge of huge energy. Everything was white with a yellow undertone and I was flooded with the energy. It physically pushed my body backwards, and for a while there was a steady vibration in my body. The floodgates opened and all the channels were filled." Those who enter the trance in stressful situations often return from it with radiant, peaceful energy.

This is considered a healing posture because the abundance of energy obtained can be extremely helpful if you have been unwell and are beginning to recuperate, though your strength is depleted. Your weakness can be physical or psychological. When I work with clients who are depressed, the first task is to clarify how the depression has served to slow them down and keep them from barreling along a life path in the wrong direction. Once the appropriate channels are identified and unclogged, the Empowerment posture can help get the life force flowing again.

As horticulturalists, the Mayans witnessed the life cycle of corn. They planted it, watched it grow from a tender young plant into maturity, then harvested it (the death cycle), saw it become the dried-up kernel with the outer appearance of death, and finally experienced it coming to life again in the Earth. The healing of self and others, and the image of corn as representative of the life, death, and regeneration cycle were all expressed in Judy's trance in the spring of 1993. Her personal healing occurred through a traditional Navajo sandpainting; it was on the wall and made of corn instead of colored sand. There were no singers, as in the traditional Navajo healing rituals, but the Corn Maidens themselves came to heal her body and her spirit. At the end she was also able to heal a friend:

> Immediately I saw a field of corn. There was a very beautiful light shining
> on it. There was a woman wandering through the field gathering corn. I
> thought, "How can this be empowering?" I then realized a single seed can
> through time create a whole field of corn. I was then standing in front of a
> huge corn sandpainting. It covered a whole wall. The sandpainting began
> to wave and shimmer. I was able to walk through the painting. Before me
> on the other side were two Corn Maidens. They were young and old at the
> same time. They had cornmeal in their hands and they spit into the corn-
> meal and began to rub me with the mixture. They looked deep within my
> spirit. I returned back through the sandpainting. I reached out and through
> Pamela and began to massage her gall bladder. I could hear the single stone
> in the rattle.

Dr. Robinette Kennedy, who did her field work on the island of Crete, identified a small statue of this posture in a standing position in the Heraklion Museum on Crete. In her work with this alternative version, she found that people tend to experience feeling taller, and there is "the suggestion of being 'perched' on a rock, log, pole, or promontory." Not only is this standing variant beneficial to those who find the kneeling position difficult to sustain, but it seems also to offer a broader perspective. One woman, using the standing position, spoke of seeing a difficult situation from a much larger historical perspective; she was thereby able to move into a position of empowerment. Another woman said she could, through her trance experience, look at power or empowerment from a place of vulnerability, and in doing so feel paradoxically strong.

DESCRIPTION

Kneel on the floor, with your heels together and your knees apart, resting your buttocks on your heels. Keeping your spine straight, raise your arms to the level of your shoulders and bend your elbows, bringing your hands together close to your chest. Curl your hands and press the knuckles together. The knuckles of one hand should fit into the spaces between the knuckles of the other hand. The back of your hands should face upward, making a flat surface from wrist to wrist, and a straight line from elbow to elbow. Keep your mouth slightly open.

THE TLAZOLTEOTL POSTURE

    The great Aztec goddess Tlazolteotl appeared, among her various manifestations, as both the Goddess of Love and the Goddess of Excrement. Some scholars suggest that the huge variety of Mesoamerican mother goddesses—who reflected the fundamental truth about life, death, and regeneration—has made it difficult to sort one from another. The figure that revealed this posture was of early origin and may have had its cultural roots in the Olmec tradition. Tlazolteotl's dual functions as Goddess

of Love and Goddess of Excrement were not so far removed as we might imagine. Among her roles as the Goddess of Love, she received the confession that each person was required to make only once, toward the conclusion of his or her life. This confession of the evil, cruel, or harmful deeds of an entire lifetime was a pouring out of verbal and emotional "filth" that, as the Goddess of Excrement, Tlazolteotl then consumed.

This tradition of "sin-eaters" was not limited to Central America. Clarissa Pinkola Estes, writing about the Bluebeard story, speaks of those spirits, birds, animals, and sometimes humans who take on the sins or the waste of the community so the people can be redeemed or cleansed.[23] It is an important function within any social group. We need sewage systems for disposing of physical waste and spiritual sewage systems for psychological waste. That is Tlazolteotl's function in this posture.

In my first experiment with this posture, I did not understand the purpose of the trance, and when a vulture appeared who wanted to eat my liver, I would not allow it. Since then, of course, I have learned to recognize and welcome the images that show me the cleansing that is taking place. So have others: "There was an eagle pecking corn. I gave it all my disabilities to dump in the volcano nearby." "I saw a raven beak going after wormlike things." "Then there was an image of the bacteria that eats grease and I was aware of it going to work on any pollution that had collected in cells throughout my body. The pollution was black and the bacteria were just working away at it throughout the rest of the trance." "I saw a PacMan gobbling up a thick, oily sludge and gray clouds of fear."

Tlazolteotl is included among the healing postures because of the obvious benefits of purification. When you use this posture, your physical body is relieved of waste you may have been unable to eliminate from your system; when it is not excreted, it becomes toxic. Likewise, your emotional body may carry around the dross of past mistakes and old hurts, which also need to be cleansed. When Judy felt terrible pain in her arms during this posture, she heard the words, "Don't endure the pain, let go of it," and she realized that the advice also applied to the emotional pain she was carrying inside.

It was a surprise to me to witness how nourishing the impurities are to Tlazolteotl. In one trance, she wiped something that looked like green petroleum jelly from inside and outside my body, then formed it into a ball. She packed it together and started to eat it, and I saw that it looked like a crunchy Rice Krispies bar. Months later, on a return trip from the recycling center, I was listening to an organic gardener extol the virtues of amaranth. This weedy, and thus easily grown, plant flourished in Central America. Its tiny black seeds were popped and mixed with honey to make a popular food, similar he said, to Rice Krispies bars. At religious rituals, the blood of those who had been sacrificed was mixed into the honey. The gardener reminded those who found this a gory and disgusting tradition that in the Christian Eucharist, the body and blood of Christ are offered for consumption by those participating in the sacrament.

Apparently even the land can be cleansed with the help of Tlazolteotl. The Cuyamungue Institute is located north of Santa Fe, and is fifteen miles downwind from Los Alamos. In one trance, I saw the cañada below the Institute property filled with dirty, sooty air. In the trance I was instructed to gather the polluted energy into a circle and to dance and sing over it. I was then shown how to dispose of the remains, finally releasing portions of the waste to each of the four elements to be safely reconstituted and restored to the Earth.

Once, while doing this posture, Carol was told, "There are many ways to be purified, and all are temporary." In the great cycles of life, things are continually turning into other things, as MaryAnna was once shown in trance. Her daughter Cindy was told, "Just relax and let the river of life flow through you." Several people were shown pools of water and a white watery substance that may have been part of the purification.

Jeff was taken on a wonderful journey in his trance using the Tlazolteotl posture:

As soon as I took my first breath during the breathing [exercise at the beginning] an extremely friendly black dog came running up to me, jumping on me, licking my face, and I knew I was to go with it. He pulled me on a sled or wagon or something and we raced through the trees to a river. We went down into the water and submerged.

The dog immediately came back. I had a strong sense of moving —
at first I thought up, but then down [in a shaft]. The black dog and I were
underwater again. We came up underground. There were two circles of
people dancing around a fire. . . . The chief came up—he had a large mask
covering his face—and asked me what I wanted. I did not know what to
say. He took me on a walk through the caves. We stopped and he put his
arm around my shoulders. He then showed me a wall that we were able to
see scenes of life on. He told me that just as the knobs could control the
scenes of life, I also had the power to control the happenings of my life
through intention and belief. He gave me his mask to look through and
then told me it was a gift for me. It would hang on my back at all times. I
can always pull it over my head to wear on my face, and looking through it
will help me see things more clearly and as they really are.

The trance concluded with his reluctant leavetaking.

Tlazolteotl is sometimes described as wearing her own decapitated
head hanging on her back. Her skull or death head is a reminder of the
inevitability of and necessity for death to keep the cycle of life, death, and
regeneration moving. With death, there is a shedding of the old, the no
longer useful parts of yourself and your life. You are reminded of who
you have been and what in you needs now to die. Tlazolteotl is always
there to receive what you are ready to relinquish. As Carol's trance message stated, "There are many ways to be purified, and all are temporary."

DESCRIPTION

*Stand with your feet parallel and your knees slightly bent. Bring your
hands together in front of your chest, and curl them so that your fingernails
face forward and point upward. (The hands of the statue seem to be holding
heavy, pendulous breasts, even though the figure is small-breasted.) Face
straight ahead. Extend your upper teeth over your lower lip, and raise your
upper lip enough that your teeth are prominently displayed.*

Divination

Divination is soothsaying—saying or revealing the truth, speaking about those secrets or mysteries that underlie the events of everyday life. Divination is the discovery of that which is hidden.

Anthropologists Lessa and Vogt define divination as the art or practice of foreseeing future events or discovering hidden knowledge through supernatural means.[24] Everyone has questions about what is going to happen in the future or why things have happened in the past. Divination by means of ecstatic trance does not involve predicting or foretelling the future, however. It is more like seeing an x-ray of a situation. You can learn through divination trances to look inside a person or a situation and see the inner structure. With the use of an x-ray in ordinary reality, you can see that a bone is broken and understand why the ankle is tender and swollen. When you understand the source of the problem, more useful remedies can be applied. Without the x-ray, you know there is a problem and you may make some good guesses about what to do; however, being able to see exactly where and how the bone is broken is invaluable information. With more specific knowledge, you know better how to respond so that healing can occur.

However, the x-ray analogy is only one perspective on divination because sometimes you may be too close to the problem. Sometimes you need some distance. Divination is also about seeing the whole pattern, the bigger picture. As one woman described it, "I go up the mountain to see the view; I am viewing a valley and all of the Earth."

I have heard fortune telling explained as the ability to get far enough away from a situation to see how it is already unfolding. Suppose you and I are climbing a mountain path. If someone who has already climbed close to the summit calls down to say there is a rock slide up ahead of us, we probably would not think it is unusual or mysterious that she would have that information. Because of her position, she has a larger perspective and can see what we are not able to see. The divination postures give that perspective.

Judy was curious about what happened to her gourd rattle, which "just that afternoon jumped off my dresser and cracked." It was the rattle she used in workshops to lead others into trance. It was special to her, a being with a spirit of its own, and she felt grief over the loss of it. She was also concerned that the "death" of the rattle meant that something was wrong, so she decided to ask the Lady of Cholula by using her posture:

> I was shown the complete cycle of the rattle's life. I saw it poke
> through the ground as a tiny sprout; I saw it mature under the hot desert
> sun; I saw it fashioned into a musical instrument and heard its beautiful
> music; I saw it split open and its life force leave, [and] I realized that the rat-
> tle had made its choice to cross over. It was a very beautiful experience. My
> sadness disappeared.

I like to include a divining posture early in an introductory workshop. From experience, I know that people who are just being introduced to ecstatic trance are more comfortable with divining than with some of the other types of trance. However, I had not considered a reason for this until I was talking with a friend about a crisis that was occurring at her workplace. She was upset, and we talked for a long time before getting ready to do a trance. We selected a metamorphosis posture because it was new to both of us and we wanted to try it.

After the rattling ended, we wrote down our experiences and she said, "Well, I sure didn't have a metamorphosis trance." I had been disappointed in my own experience as well, which had brought me only to the edge of metamorphosis. "We should have done a divining posture," I said, without even thinking about it. "Divination is focused on what's going on in our world, in the Middle World. It takes us into the Alternate

Reality that is connected with the world we live in so that we can see it from a different perspective."

Native societies understood the power of divination as coming from contact with Alternate Reality. Through the altered state of consciousness of the trance and the ritual of body posture to frame the experience, you are able to move out of the limitations of ordinary perception. The world of the spirits, magical because it is unseen in ordinary awareness, becomes available. You move into that larger world, stretch your sensory capacities, and see and hear what is always there, all the time. The trance is powerful not because it takes you away, but because it lets you be more completely present where you already are. That may seem magical. To me, it just lets me know how incredibly rich and beautiful the Middle World, which is my current home, really is.

Most people are more familiar with scrying methods of divination—reading messages in the innards of animals sacrificed for that purpose, or tossing stones. Many know about divination through the *I Ching*, the Chinese Book of Changes, in which you identify the characteristics of the times by tossing three coins six times. The Wilhelm/Baynes translation of the *I Ching* includes a concise description of Carl Jung's notion of synchronicity as an explanation for divination. Jung defined synchronicity as "a concept that formulates a point of view diametrically opposed to that of causality."[25] Simply put, the principle of synchronicity suggests that there is a quality or characteristic of a moment can be extracted from any of a variety of experiences; this quality can be read in cards or coins or daydreams, which become metaphors for the larger issues playing out at the same time.

In any case, none of these explanations rely on anything "super"-natural, as Lessa and Vogt's earlier definition states. Divination is as natural as seeing, if you will expand your worldview to contain a large enough context for the events of your life.

It is important to prepare well for a divining trance. Whatever you perceive in Alternate Reality must be filtered through your personal consciousness, the intellectual and emotional processing of your personal self. In a workshop I attended some years ago with Helen Palmer, a practiced teacher of intuition development, she talked about the importance of learning to discriminate between feedback from the mind and feedback from the intuition. The art of discrimination involves learning how to empty yourself. Palmer is a student and practitioner of Zen, and she applies her experience with meditation to this process of emptying. In order to function well as a diviner, you too must learn to empty your mind and then to distinguish thoughts from intuitive perceptions.

I do not mean to say that what we experience in trance is not real, only that we perceive it through our psychological filters. Three people on vacation in Paris will have three different stories to tell about the trip, even if they remain side by side every moment. A student of architecture will see the street scene differently from someone who is falling in love with the person walking along beside him or her. Of course each of us perceives things differently. The point is just to be aware of the filter that makes every perception somewhat subjective.

In my practice as a psychologist, I often work with dreams. I believe that in order to understand dreams or divination experiences, it is helpful to share the information with at least one other person, rather than trying to interpret it on your own. You can be too close to the issue, unable to see the forest for the trees, or too invested in one view of a situation. Sometimes, just in the reading or telling of a trance, you can hear in your choice of words a meaning to the events or perceptions that eluded you while you were experiencing them. And sometimes another person brings a different set of assumptions or associations to the material. Try telling a friend about a dream or trance experience, and compare your respective responses and interpretations.

There are three criteria you can use for determining if an interpretation of a dream is correct. First, an accurate reading of the dream usually produces an "Aha," a feeling in your gut that the meaning rings true. Second, the experience either tells you something you did not already know or reminds you of something you have forgotten. And third, you are usually emotionally affected. You may break into a smile or tears, or feel a visceral change once the meaning is understood. These criteria can guide your understanding of divination trances also.

You can use the following guidelines to help you decide which divining trance to use. The Adena Pipe posture is especially useful for asking questions about health and healing—for individuals, groups, animals, or the land. The Hunter Diviner posture is physically difficult, so many people tend not to use it. It was originally used to search for game; you can use it to ask where you are going or to find something you seek. Consulting the Lady of Cholula or the Tennessee Diviner postures is like seeking advice from old friends or relatives. The Lady of Cholula is like a wise grandmother who is kind and nurturing, yet can be blunt when plain speaking is called for. The Tennessee Diviner is like an old curmudgeon who is often terse regarding personal matters, but when asked about ritual, becomes eloquent. The Nupe Mallam posture is the one you can use to ask about matters concerning social relationships or problem situations within a group. The Olmec Diviner, a new posture, gives a cool, objective perspective, helping you learn about something rather than giving you answers.

THE ADENA PIPE POSTURE

My first encounter with the Adena Pipe posture was in Hawaii, a number of years ago. I was already alert to finding postures as I wandered through museums, and I came back from that trip eager to try this new position. However, the group I was working with in Ohio had other new postures, and this one was put at the bottom of the pile. A few years later we came across the same posture, this time on a figure in a publication from the Ohio Historical Society. It was identified as a stone pipe effigy

unearthed from a funeral mound belonging to the Adena Indians, the Moundbuilders who lived in central and southern Ohio 2000 years ago.

My body felt very powerful when I squared my shoulders and thrust back my pelvis to assume the position of the little stone pipe. The power I felt was described well in an article written by a body-awareness instructor, Dr. Paul Linden. He wrote about his work with survivors of childhood sexual abuse:

> I showed her that the ease and stability of the stance depends on rotating the pelvis in the opposite [open] direction and arching the back a bit. She found that very threatening because it held her anus and vagina wide-open and accessible. In order to make that position endurable, I showed her a breathing exercise for cultivating a sense of dense, fiery power. . . . We kept working with the stance until she could stay in her wide-open position and maintain her stability of breathing. . . . She felt that closing and constricting herself reduced her power and that she was most powerful and effective when she felt most vulnerable. That paradoxical piece of understanding gave her a whole new view of how she would have to confront her past pain. . . . The issue of vulnerability is a crucial one for survivors of abuse, and it is important for them to *experience* (emphasis mine) that being wide-open allows them to perceive and act in a freer, more powerful way.[26]

In this posture, you are wide open in your lower chakras. I would like to suggest that the flow of energy from the planet, characteristic in all the standing and many of the sitting postures, is enhanced and therefore more powerful in the Adena Pipe posture. MaryAnna, for instance, reported, "My thighs seemed to grow bigger and I had chills"; later she added, "Last night I noticed an increase in energy, and even this morning I had extra energy—up and ready to go at 5:00 a.m." It is common for me to have my body vibrate in this posture during trance. I recorded the following experience in my notes:

> [I was getting a lot of information and] along the way began to ask ques-
> tions to confirm my perceptions, and my knees shook, my body shook, there
> was light in my head and heat—the intensity of my reaction seemed a way to
> convey the intensity of the confirmation (of the accuracy of the messages I was
> receiving). . . . The intensity of the shaking rose—I was so hot and needed all
> my focus to remain in the posture. . . . I thought it would never be over and
> was exhausted, but now I am energized, except for the heat still in my face.

Clearly this posture can be strenuous. In order for this degree of openness to be safe, it is important to undertake the trance in the context of ritual. By preparing yourself, inviting the help of the spirits, entering trance on cue, and leaving on cue, you protect yourself from receiving more energy than you are able to manage.

In our earliest experiments with the Adena Pipe posture in Columbus, we did not know that its purpose was divining and did not ask questions, still ignorant of its special usage. One woman found herself in a desert and for a very long time had the feeling she was supposed to be hunting, although nothing occurred. What a lovely metaphor to prompt her! She was supposed to be hunting, for an answer or an understanding, but was instead in a barren desert because there was no question; it was an empty space in which to look for something. The divining capacity of this posture was revealed another way in one of Judy's trances:

> I also saw a crystal suspended in the center of us. It sparkled out rain-
> bow colors. When I got up close to the crystal, I could look into each facet,
> and each was a piece of the story. I could look into one facet and something
> would be going on, and then I could move to another and something dif-
> ferent would be happening.

While clearly a divining posture, the Adena Pipe is especially useful for asking questions about health and healing. Carol, in one of her early

experiences, had the presence of mind to ask for help from her animal spirit friends. She called on the bear and eagle to help her get light into the bodies of two people who were ill. Later, when she saw that one of them was being held back, she asked the bear and the wolf to help. When you use the Adena Pipe posture, clearly ask a question pertaining to healing, that is, to helping a person, animal, organization, or family become more whole. Once the question has been posed, then it is helpful to ask those spirit beings who have previously befriended you to help you see and understand the dynamics that need to change. Others have seen the influx of energy to support that change as the presence of thousands of birds, or a mountain meadow full of hundreds of Monarch butterflies.

The fact that healing involves balancing can be illustrated in trance by images of daylight and darkness, the sun and the moon, energy flows on the right and left sides of the body, or, as one person saw, a shaman standing half in sunlight and half in moonlight, "separated right down the middle, and he was rattling."

DESCRIPTION

Stand with your feet parallel, about eight inches apart; note that in this stance your feet are farther apart than in the usual standing posture. Bend your knees, and tilt your pelvis so that your buttocks stick out in the back. Try bending forward from the hips, then straightening your torso without moving your hips. Square your shoulders, your arms held stiffly away from your body, your fingers pointing toward the ground. In the Hawaiian version of this posture, the thumbs are held away from the fingers, forming a "U" between the forefingers and the thumbs. Face straight ahead with your mouth slightly opened, but do not make any sound. As always, close your eyes.

The Hunter Diviner Posture

The oldest postures, which come extant from the hunter-gatherers, are often terribly difficult to hold for even fifteen minutes. It is humbling to realize that a few hours a week working out at the health club or gardening or hiking are insufficient to keep a person in shape for standing in just one position for such a short time. The ancient hunter gatherers used their bodies rather than machines for transportation and work. They were muscular and lean and supple. Perhaps for the hunter-gatherer diviners, it was not so excruciating to stand in this posture, with their arms at right angles to their bodies. There are pictures of them everywhere, from Australian rock art to Siberian images drawn on the walls of caves. I especially like one Siberian drawing: elongated antennae extend from the diviner's head, arms, torso, and feet. This was a clever way for the hunter gatherers to express the enhanced sensitivity acquired in this trance—the ability to perceive energy fields at a great distance.

This trance is best used for asking where to find something. Your questioning can be geographical, like Jackie asking where she should look for a new apartment. Be prepared for a terse answer. When Jackie asked, "What about a place to live?" she was told that she already knew, so why ask. Instead of seeing a location for a home, she saw herself actually becoming a house. One possible interpretation of this image, the one meaningful to her, was that she would not find what she was looking for by moving to a new apartment, but rather by finding a new way to live within herself.

Your question can also focus on locating something. For example, Judith asked to find the source of her fibromyalgia. She was actively shaken throughout her trance, "with the rattle and drum telling me how to do it." She saw a translucent egg that had never formed its shell, and inside it, a beating heart. The fragile egg needed warmth and nutrients, which were provided in "the milk of corn . . . beams of sun . . . and the feminine embodiment of the wind that wraps the warmth of the sun around the egg." A combination of body movement and exquisite imagery gave Judith the answer to her question about her muscular pain.

This is a difficult posture. I have not asked the Hunter Diviner many questions, so I have few reports to share. I have a hunch, though, that like the other ancient and difficult poses, this one offers great beauty

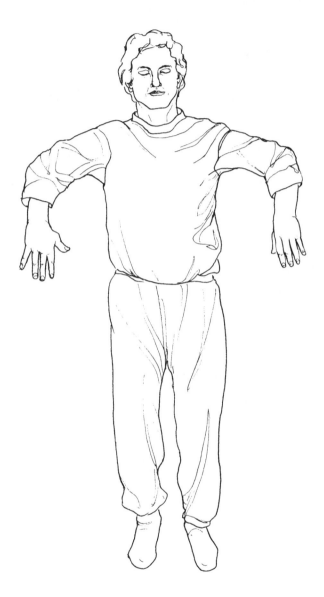

to those who would endure. Using this posture, I once asked about a relationship, wanting to see where it was going. The answer came in these poetic words: "Be steady and true. It will take time but it is worth it all, and in the end we will see the exquisite beauty of the pattern that has been and is being woven throughout our lives."

Your perceptions during trance may be affected by the knowledge that this posture was used by hunters. Its purpose is so deeply linked with finding game that even city dwellers have experiences that are relevant to the life of the hunters. People see wide landscapes and herds of running animals. Others speak of being very watchful. Spirals of wind, sound, or energy are common, and the spirits that come to help are sometimes in the form of a large black bird or "clothed in fine layers of gold cloth."

DESCRIPTION

The original posture involves a very difficult stance. Your feet are about a foot apart, with your left toes pointing toward the left and your right toes pointing toward the right; your knees are bent. If this is not possible for you to achieve (and hold for fifteen minutes!), then the usual standing position works as well. That is, stand with your feet parallel, about six inches apart, your toes pointing straight ahead. Your knees should be slightly bent. Square your shoulders. Extend your arms straight out to the side, your right arm extending right, your left arm extending left. Keeping your elbows at shoulder level, drop your lower arms, so that they hang down from your elbows, with the palms of your hands facing backward. Stretch the fingers of your hands as wide as they will extend. Face straight ahead with your eyes closed.

THE LADY OF CHOLULA POSTURE

What a treasure it is to have a friend who is older and wiser, who gladly sits with you to talk about whatever puzzles you, who somehow always puts the confusion of the moment into some perspective. You may have had a grandparent who was just such a friend. In the other reality, the Lady of Cholula is a wise old grandmother who can lovingly set things straight for you and, if necessary, be sufficiently blunt and uncompromising to keep you from wallowing in the problems that have become comfortable little ruts.

Those of us at the Cuyamungue Institute have always called this spirit being the *Lady* of Cholula. As I was collecting my information to write about her, I questioned whether it might not be more politically correct to call her the *Woman* of Cholula. To me, the term lady implies white gloves and tea parties, or a frustrated mother's admonition to her active daughter to "learn to act like a lady." It also implies a hierarchical social structure, harkening back to the days of the lord and lady of the manor. When I posed this question to Dr. Goodman, however, she informed me that it was a practice of early anthropologists to address each older Indian woman as "Lady." It was, in fact, considered highly disrespectful to speak of a venerable grandmother as a "woman," whether from Cholula or anywhere else. With that in mind, and in keeping with honoring medieval personages like the Lady of the Lake from the Arthurian legends, I have retained her title as the Lady of Cholula.

Cholula was an important pre-Hispanic religious center in the Puebla province of central Mexico. It was established by the Toltecs and later became an Aztec city devoted to the worship of Quetzalcoatl. Anthropologists found two female figures in Cholula dating from around A.D. 1350. They were seated in the Lady of Cholula posture; both were wearing the same pointed hats and the same collars with tassles, and both were sitting on stools. Some years ago, Dr. Goodman replicated the hat and collar and gave them to me as presents on my birthday. She brought her own set, so we each wore a hat and collar as we tried this posture for the first time. Our experience that evening showed us that the hat and collar enhance the practitioner's ability to focus and hence improve the clarity of the vision. This has been confirmed on many other occasions.

To understand the characteristics of a particular posture, it is best to refer to personal encounters. MaryAnna asked about "the stages to take in getting our own farm." She recounted:

> I kept yawning at the beginning. An owl came to me as soon as the trance started, out of the darkness. Then I saw a white shimmering dragonfly, which changed into a butterfly that touched me then flew away. I received the words "seeing is not seeing, feeling is seeing." Then the thoughts of finding the right place and direction to go would be through my feelings. I was told that the right place may not look right but that I would be given a sign. The smell and taste of strawberries would be strong. I would not remember this sign until it happened. Then I saw a figure with a beautiful wild-flower wreath around her head. I asked for more help and the words from before were repeated.

The exact wording of the question determines the response. When MaryAnna asked a question about the *next* step to take in reaching her goal, the Lady of Cholula gave her pictures of fixing dinner that night in her apartment. Her interpretation was that the *next* step was to go fix dinner and get on with living in the present, knowing that she would arrive at her goal by always taking the next step that lay just in front of her.

In all of the divining postures, people tend to receive answers both in images and words. It is not unusual for someone to hear a distinct message, such as, "seeing is not seeing, feeling is seeing." Perhaps that is one reason people respond so strongly to the Lady of Cholula and the Tennessee Diviner as very real beings; they speak to people in words, and they have identifiable personality styles. This sense of personality occurs more readily the more familiar a person becomes with the posture and hence with the spirit being who is represented in the clay figures. Newcomers are more likely to have physical sensations and images that relate to their questions. Nancy, concerned about her physical wellbeing, asked, "What do I need to be whole?" She experienced a lot of jerking in her body as though she were falling asleep. This raised a question for her about how conscious she really was during her everyday living, or, in other words, to what extent she was both here and not here. She felt heat in her hands, her spine, and her forehead, perhaps as her increased awareness aided the life force flowing through her body.

Other newcomers fight the trance, not sure they really want to know the answers to the questions once they are posed. John asked what would be happening to him professionally. He became very tired; his left hand went numb; and he wanted more than anything for the rattling to be over. While his body moved to the sound of the rattle, he saw a glyph like a snake, then experienced a fear of going away—of something that was going to happen and then didn't. He knew in the trance that he was fearful and was trying too hard, and that beneath his nagging doubt, something else was going on. At the time, he was unwilling to know what that "something else" might be.

Recently a woman called me, concerned because she had had a trance experience in which the bear, who had befriended her in previous trances, had come to her baring his teeth. She was worried, having read in *The Way of the Shaman*[27] that if one meets a snarling animal in Alternate Reality to walk away. Then I learned that this event had occurred during a divining trance, when she had asked the Lady of Cholula about the direction she should take with her education and career. She had mentioned feeling betrayed by the bear, and I asked her if she was experiencing a sense of betrayal in her ordinary reality life. It came as no surprise to me that this was indeed her perception of her current circumstances. This awareness alone cleared up a lot of her confusion.

However, the woman still had the question of what to do about encountering a snarling animal. Teachers of specific traditions offer prescriptions from those traditions for dealing with particular problems. Since these postures come from a wide array of cultures with differing traditions, and because there are not religious specialists from all these traditions to act as guides and teachers, there is no list of specific things to look for or particular responses that are always correct. I gave the woman two suggestions. I told her to first ask a friend to go with her as

she journeyed into Alternate Reality. Perhaps it would be wise for her to use the ritual body postures with a partner or a group, at least for awhile. More importantly, I also suggested she ask a spirit friend to accompany her—another animal spirit who consistently helped her in trance. It seemed simple and straightforward. If I were traveling to Afghanistan, a very unknown territory for me, and I knew someone who lived there, I would ask that friend to travel with me. In the unknown realms of Alternate Reality, I ask my spirit friends to help me find my way, to protect me from my own ignorance.

Secondly, I suggested to the woman that she use the same common sense in Alternate Reality that guided her in ordinary reality. If I met a snarling bear on a hike in the mountains, I would not pursue her or challenge her. She might have cubs nearby she was protecting. Whatever the reason, I would respect her message that I had intruded where I did not belong. This would not mean she had the intention to hurt me; I would only be in danger to the extent that I did not pay attention and behave respectfully. My years of experiencing ecstatic trance and facilitating workshops have led me to believe that this is also true when I travel in the other realms.

I was a little frightened myself not long ago, one evening when I was alone and had asked the Lady of Cholula for some help. During the trance, I heard the door to my room creak a little and was distinctly aware of a presence in the room. With my eyes closed, it seemed as though a shadow passed in front of the candles before me. I had to laugh at myself. Although I speak of the Lady of Cholula as being very real to me, when it came to finding her in the room with me, I got scared. We are always treading lightly on the line that divides the two worlds: ordinary life and nonordinary, sacred reality. We must be prepared for those occasions when the two worlds meet in the same room.

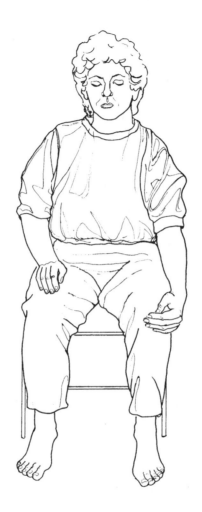

DESCRIPTION

A chair is required for this posture. Sit in the chair with your legs apart and your feet pointed straight ahead. Cup your left hand around the front of your left knee. Rest your right hand palm down with the fingers forward on your right leg, just above the knee and slightly to the right. Your left arm, then, is somewhat tensed as it is pulled forward, while your right arm is more relaxed. Depending on the height of the chair and the length of your legs, it

may be necessary to put a cushion under your feet to raise them. Lean forward slightly, with your spine straight, and bend forward from the hip joint. Hold your head straight, with your eyes closed, looking forward. Your tongue should protrude gently from between your lips.

The clay figure of this posture shows the Lady of Cholula wearing a hat and collar. The hat is cone-shaped and pointed, with "fingers" radiating from the base. The collar is circular, extending over her shoulders, chest, and back. These props may heighten or intensify your trance.

THE NUPE MALLAM POSTURE

Mallam is the word for "diviner" among the Nupe, a tribe in sub-Saharan Africa. The only evidence of this posture is a photograph showing a man seated in this position. No artworks have been identified from this or any other area of the world that illustrate the same pose. Among those who have experienced it, the Nupe Mallam posture is rarely referred to affectionately or with humor. The spirit being of this posture seems so much more detached and dispassionate than the other diviners. It is as though, for this diviner, a wide perspective is always taken for granted, a perspective from which the whole pattern of social relationships is revealed. As discussed in the introduction to this chapter, divination is not used for predicting the future; the Nupe Mallam posture is consulted for help in understanding a current predicament or to answer a problem.

One woman asked the Nupe Mallam for help in learning to accept her personal power. She wrote: "As I became aware of the double rattle, [indicating to her that she was in trance], I felt surges of power, clear, holding nothing back. I felt the purity of that power; there was no cruelty or brutality, just a pure experience and an expression of a quality." She was learning, as another participant commented, that the answers often come through "being." She was learning by having her body and emotions exist together in a new way, rather than by knowing something in an exclusively intellectual manner. In my psychology practice, I work with several body-oriented therapists. We have continual discussions about the importance of shifting the center of experiencing to a new level so that it becomes possible to respond differently to the accustomed events in life. Divining trances can provide just that shift—an unplanned excursion into an alternate mode of being in the ordinary world. This woman discovered her hidden fear that she would become cruel or brutal with her power, and because of that fear she had held back all expressions of her personal power. In trance she was free from the filtering action of her ego. She felt the quality of power. Now she had a guide, an inner standard against which to compare future surges of power: if the power had a good quality, she could let it flow; if not, she could still hold it back—but now she knew how to compare, and now she had a choice.

Similarly, another woman who was anticipating a few major life changes asked how to best prepare for those changes. In response to her question, the trance took her on a speeding underground train. It was like a roller coaster taking her from one terrifying experience to the next.

However, in the end she discovered that she survived. At the conclusion of the trance, she knew more about the pattern she was enacting in her life. More importantly, she knew she could survive the stress of the major life changes because she experienced a successful conclusion to her harrowing ride.

Sometimes the guidance is more visual. I asked to be shown what direction to take in a career change I was considering. The Nupe Mallam trance showed me an etching that had hung in my living room for ten years. In the actual print, there is a craggy mountain and a path leading the way to a huge tree, which is for me the Tree of Life. In the trance, as I was traveling on the road, everything on either side of it began to fall away. Soon there was nothing else but the road. I realized with a smile that there was no longer a question about which path to take, for now there was only one path. I was content in my journey toward the wonderful tree.

Sometimes even a timeline is spelled out. A member of the group in Columbus was told in a March workshop that by the end of the summer she would know what steps to take in her marriage. The following August she met an old friend while on vacation. This friend helped her sort out what was missing in her relationship with her husband, and on returning home, they began marriage counseling. This could be construed as prediction, but perhaps it is not fortunetelling any more than a prediction that the roses will blossom in June. Maybe there are seasons and patterns in life that are well known to those who live in the timeless realms. From witnessing the cycling of lives and relationships many times, the spirits can share the wisdom of their perspective without diminishing in any way our ability and responsibility to choose for ourselves.

Like the Tennessee Diviner, the Nupe Mallam is sometimes known to give concise answers. Dawn asked, "Where should I look for new friends?" and she was shown empty desolate places, desert landscapes, and cliffs. Nancy wanted to know what would benefit her relationship with

her children, and she heard, repeated in the rattle like a mantra, "Listen, listen, listen." Janet asked about work and became an animal being run down by a bigger faster animal. I didn't understand the meaning of her image when I first heard her describe it, but that too was revealed in trance. The words she heard were, "Be careful not to be run down by the mania at work."

This posture can assist you in physically gaining an answer or a confirmation of an understanding. As you sit in this position, you use your left arm as a rigid support for your body. People report knowing that they are drawing energy up from the Earth through that arm. Sometimes in trance they describe poles for accomplishing the same transfer of energy.

Or more poetically, there is a figure that rises through the arm and subtly speaks into the left ear of the diviner. You may experience spinning or twirling sensations at the outset of this trance, followed by feeling that you are split open or otherwise opened up. The quality of finding out or understanding may be experienced either through digging into something or through achieving an overview. You may see an image of piercing a veil or seeking a light at the end of a tunnel. Or you may stand on a mountaintop or fly with an eagle. The Nupe Mallam posture will help you see in a new way.

DESCRIPTION

Sit on the floor, leaning toward your left and supported by your left arm. Hold your left arm rigid, with your hand at a right angle to your body. Place your left hand at a spot three to five inches to the left of your body and just behind a straight line drawn along the back of your buttocks. Bend both legs at the knees, with both feet pointing to the right, positioned so that your left foot is resting just to the left of your right knee. Place your right hand on your lower left leg, where the muscle indents about halfway down your calf. Move your head slightly to the left, so you are looking over your left knee, and close your eyes.

If a knee injury or other cause of discomfort requires you to do so, you can accomplish this trance facing the opposite direction—that is, in a mirror image of the position described above.

THE OLMEC DIVINER POSTURE

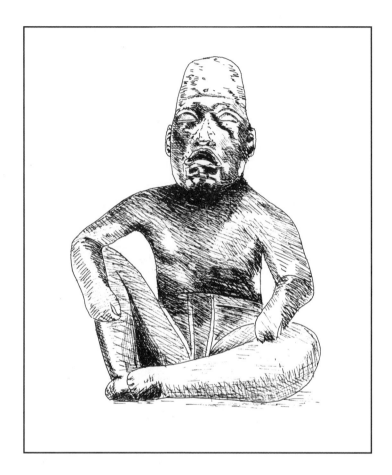

Those of us who have utilized the ritual postures for a while have attuned our eyes to carvings and drawings that hold a promise of ritual use. While going through her mother's belongings following her death, Elizabeth found a photograph of a seated figure carved in jade. His elongated head and drooping mouth were unmistakeably Olmec, and the precise placement of his hand on his inner leg told her that this was surely a ritual posture. She brought the photograph to a birthday party for Dr. Goodman. At this annual event, we have a tradition of trying out a new ritual posture before the birthday dinner, and this Olmec posture was the one selected for the occasion.

There was no information about the origins of this posture. Because the photograph appeared to be a page from a magazine, Elizabeth wrote to the Smithsonian Museum, then followed up on a lead with the curator of the Dumbarton Oaks collection. No one recognized the carving, so we were on our own in finding out the purpose of this specific posture. There were thirteen of us at the birthday party, mostly oldtimers at ecstatic trance. After we performed the posture, an array of experiences were told, but the specific purpose of the posture was not clear. This was to be expected in a field that is highly experimental, and in which we are led and guided by those in the other realms.

Many of us were taken by this posture to the edge of our known world, to the stratosphere or the brink of death, or deep into the innards of animals. However, I found my first real clue to the possible purpose of this posture when I paid attention to its physical characteristics. The bent legs and placement of hands were similar to the Lady of Cholula and Tennessee Diviner postures. When I reread the reports I received from others who tried the posture at the birthday party, there were several characteristics that pointed to its being a divining posture.

In our experiences, there was an emphasis on perspective, suggesting that, in lieu of specific questions, we were being guided toward understanding how to gain perspective on particular situations. There were references to going inside. Carol went into an Arabian or medieval tent; Kathleen entered a dark cave. Going into something was a metaphorical image for shifting to the inner dimensions of a situation—getting to the heart or guts of the matter. There were also images of getting really close to the minutiae, or moving far away to get the big picture. One person described "going into an ant house and watching them working, then flying above the trees and watching the Earth get tiny." Elizabeth climbed to a very high platform, and MaryAnna looped up into the stratosphere. I experienced being out in the great void and looking in on life.

Learning from this diviner is experiential, as with all the divination postures. Pamela said about her trance:

> Then I was back again with the animals, insects, and plants—tiny again—and they were all gathered around as though telling me something about their destruction. I became full-sized and realized how much life was killed by just walking in the grass. I got small again and was back in the circle and telling them [about what she had just learned]. The circle of life, the laws of nature, and—they said to me—even so with man is death.

Six weeks earlier, halfway across the country, I too had had a vision of death. In the trance I was a gatherer of medicinal plants and was traveling to a nearby tribe to take herbs to them:

> As I cross the river, I am thinking that when I die my soul will fly like a bird to the sun. Then I am lying, dying, in a cool dark hut. My body has been covered with large boiled leaves that calm down my nervous system. This helps my physical body sensations slow down so that as I die it will be easy for me to get out of my body. My breathing becomes very slow, my heartbeat slow. I say to myself that when the rattle stops I will die and fly to the sun. Then my observing ego realizes it is not time for me to die in my physical body and I had better not continue in this way, so in the trance I become instead a younger woman sitting in a group that surrounds an older dying woman. The group is gathered there to support her as she dies. Now as the younger woman, I know I will become the gatherer of healing herbs, and that one day I will die in the same way. My mind asks, "Why? Why do we go through this continual round of living, healing, dying?" And the rattle stops. I got no answer.

Several participants commented about feeling cool. When Dr. Goodman read the reports of the group that had first tried this posture, she suggested that it may mediate a spirit journey trance, since people often feel cold during a spirit journey. I did another trance to ask if this was indeed a divining posture. The answer to the question was not clear. The response seemed to be more about me—about an opportunity to learn more about myself, and especially my hidden shadow parts. In the trance, I wondered if perhaps this posture was not for asking general questions *but for learning about something (including myself)*. There was a sound of the muffled clapping of hands in the background and a little voice saying, "Yes, Yes, Yes." Only further experience with the Olmec Diviner posture will determine if he is a diviner after all.

DESCRIPTION

Sit on the floor in a cross-legged fashion. Keep your left leg resting on the floor and draw your right knee up so that your arm can lean on it. Place your right foot sole down on the floor, with the sole of your left foot perpendicular to it and resting against your right foot. Cup your left hand and rest it on the inside of your leg, at the knee. Hold your arm rigid, slightly away from your body. Extend your right arm so that your right elbow rests on your right kneecap and your forearm hangs down your shin. Relax your hand, with your fingers slightly curled. Stare straight ahead, your eyes closed and your mouth slightly open.

THE TENNESSEE DIVINER POSTURE

A figure of a little man in this posture was found in a gravesite in Wilson County, Tennessee. Similar figures were found in wooden temples atop earthen mounds in the same part of the country. They date from about A.D. 700. The little man from the gravesite is almost naked, but he wears a distinctive cap that fits close to his head and has a tail hanging down along the cervical vertebrae of his neck. His face is ceremonially painted, with a line drawn from one earlobe across the bridge of his nose to the opposite earlobe.

I especially love doing this posture in the kiva at the Cuyamungue Institute. The group of us that gathers to consult the Tennessee Diviner lies down on the floor of this circular building with our heads in the center and our bodies extending like spokes of a wheel. Dr. Goodman quietly approaches us one by one, kneeling over us and drawing the ceremonial face with a black greasepaint crayon. We lie down as people from the ordinary world and we rise changed into beings prepared to cross the line into other realms.

The spirit being who is the Tennessee Diviner is notoriously sardonic and short tempered, and it is always best to summon him respectfully and to thank him afterward for lending his assistance. His messages in response to personal questions are likely to be brief and even cryptic. However, given the opportunity to participate in the creation of ritual, which is his forte, he is generous with exacting details that may be repeated during the trance to assure accuracy.

The Tennessee Diviner posture is demanding in a very physical way as well. It is one of the most uncomfortable of the postures because it is hard to stay balanced sitting on one foot with your other leg raised; your left foot inevitably goes to sleep. Typically when the rattling ends, the groans begin. The only encouragement is to use the pain as a reminder to focus on the rattle, for in trance the pain is no longer a problem. My colleagues joke about shifting into that altered state as soon as we can in order to escape the physical discomfort of the ordinary world.

Because of the Tennessee Diviner's love of ritual, this posture is always included in the Masked Trance Dance workshops to ask for the rituals that serve as the focal points of the dance. In these workshops, we begin by journeying to the Lower World to encounter animal spirits who will befriend us. Our purpose is to create masks and costumes of those animal spirit friends so that, at the culmination of a workshop, we can have a metamorphosis dance. Like the Pueblo Indians do in the animal dances of the American Southwest—the Deer Dance, Buffalo Dance, and Eagle Dance—we pay our respects to the spirits who wear the animal masks, and in return we are invited to become those animals for a brief time. We ask the Tennessee Diviner for guidance about the rituals that lead up to the trance state of the metamorphosis. Over the years, we have discovered that the rituals form stories that come from the mythic realms—archetypal stories that restore our deepest memories of other ways of being and knowing.

Each Masked Trance Dance is different; each brings a distinct story from the other reality. They are surprising in their relevance. In the early summer of 1991, a small group of eight gathered at the Cuyamungue Institute. During a morning trip to the Lower World using the Sami posture, we were befriended by the animals whose masks we would create during the week. That afternoon we gathered again in the kiva, this time to ask the Tennessee Diviner, "What should our dance be about? How should it be done?"

I was chosen to wear the special cap that Dr. Goodman had created to duplicate the one worn by the Tennessee Diviner figure. Experience had shown that wearing it tended to enhance the clarity and intensity of the trance, but it was not necessary to have a cap or to make facial markings across the cheeks and nose in order to accomplish the trance. Only one cap had been made, so our group had to determine which of the eight of us would be singled out to wear it. The method of choosing was a Hungarian children's rhyme, a version of "Eenie, meenie, miney, mo" that is still unpronounceable to my thick tongue. I think it was the first time I had ever worn the cap in the ten years I had been visiting Alternate Reality with the ritual postures. I thought I should pose some weighty questions about the board meeting planned later that week, but when I asked about these practical matters, there was no response.

When the rattling started, I saw dancers with skirts and wide, black-and-white feather headdresses in a circle, dancing close to the ground out in the driveway (just a big open space beyond the kiva), but there was a pueblo in the background. They were dancing around a fire where Dr. Goodman placed the rock that looks like a mountain lion. There were also fires at the sweatlodge and in the center of the dance court. The three fires made a big triangle. At one point there was a vision of Gwyn, wearing her gorgeous mountain goat mask, leading us to the sweatlodge. I saw us feeding all the fires:

> I see a ritual in the kiva. We are all sitting in a circle. Each of us, fully masked and costumed, takes a turn sitting in the middle of the circle while the others touch us so that we may receive healing. We are each chosen by an animal spirit that needs healing: whale, dolphin, bear, wolf, turtle, owl, mountain goat. In the trance I ask if this is correct, and I receive a surge of energy and my body becomes rigid while my head fills with light. Afterward I am still very hot.

Of course, the six other participants also had visions or trances to contribute to the overall understanding of the dance. Elliot saw waves of flowers covering the whole plaza as a reminder to do the dance for the sake of the dance itself. Allison brought a spirit of playfulness: a dolphin riding the waves and dancing in flames. She was told that the dance was about power and learning to lovingly bring all that we feel to the moment of speaking. Robinette saw an Indian brave dancing down a tunnel, his dance gorgeous and his energy exciting. In this dance was a balance between male and female, and a message for the bear. Gwyn saw dancing at the base of the Tree of the World, which split and had to be healed, the parts reunited. Sally was given some very specific dance steps and a vision of a ceremonial gateway to mark our entrance into the other world at the dance. As the owl, she asked each of us, "Whooo are you?" and we each stepped forward to speak our names, both human and animal, to be acknowledged in the spirit world. Barb saw the cycle of water as it changed from clouds to rain to waterfall to ocean and back to clouds again.

What did we make of all this variety? As we analyzed the details of each person's trance, the richness of a dance emerged from what the Tennessee Diviner had given us. There was a general layout of the dance, places to perform each segment, and choreography of very specific dance steps. There were messages of wisdom like those received by Elliot and Allison to guide us. And throughout all the trances was an awareness of pain and tragedy to be healed in the world.

The recurring fires in my trance were later explained as the remnants of the Persian Gulf War that had scarred the planet earlier that year. In a trance later that week, I witnessed the pain and terror and horror resulting from all the atrocities. When I told the others, who were in their animal forms, they told me they too had seen all the horrors I had witnessed. But now it was time to heal.

The old diviner led us into a mythic story that was alive in our present world—the story of wars and fires of destruction; the story of witnessing the horror; and the story of healing. In the wake of all that had harmed the planet and her animal and human children, it was possible for us to be part of the restoration, the healing of the split in the Tree of the World. It was possible for us to experience doing our part. Behind his crusty demeanor, I imagine that the Tennessee Diviner smiled.

DESCRIPTION

Begin in a kneeling position, with your buttocks resting on your heels. Now raise your right knee and place your right foot sole down on the floor, beside your left knee. In order to hold this position for fifteen minutes, it may be helpful to put a pillow between your left buttock and left leg. Rest your left hand, palm down, on your left knee, and your right hand on your right knee,

but slightly to the left. Cock your head very slightly to the right, as if you are wanting to look over your right knee, but keep your eyes closed. Protrude your tongue slightly from between your lips.

The figure from Tennessee wears a cap that fits close to his head. It has a strip of material down the middle of the head that forms a tail that extends along the cervical vertebrae of his neck. Two circles mark spots on each side of his scalp from which, as one person suggested, horns might grow. Small flaps make sideburns, and the cap is cut out over his ears. Our experience at the

Cuyamungue Institute indicates that wearing such a cap helps the wearer to focus, intensifying the trance. It is important to remove the cap as soon as the trance has ended.

Whether wearing the cap or not, we occasionally adopt the practice of replicating the line painted across the Tennessee Diviner figure's face. If you choose to do this, use a greasepaint crayon to draw a black line from one earlobe across the bridge of your nose to the other earlobe.

Metamorphosis

We are horticulturalists. Like the hunter gatherers who came before us, the men of our small village still hunt local game to supplement our food supply, but mostly we are fed from the gardens planted and tended by the women. Because we need to be close to our gardens, to care for the plants and harvest them, we remain in the same place and do not follow the game. Our homes are more permanent structures than those of the hunter gatherers, no longer designed to be quickly disassembled and packed up for moves to different locations. The ways we interact socially are also different from those of our ancestors. There are more rules to govern how we live together. These rules teach us the value of reciprocity, of giving and receiving equally so that harmony and balance are maintained within the community.

Our women, by observing the cycles of plant life when gathering roots and fruits and berries, learned to cultivate plants in gardens of their own. Yet, with all that we have learned, something has been lost. We were once an integral part of nature, flowing with the same rhythms that affected the birds, forests, animals, and sea. Now that we have learned to control a small portion of nature, we have lost some of that mystical unity with the natural world.

Stories are told of the time when the boundaries separating humans from animals were soft and could stretch. This ease of communing with the animals is a memory of past times, told by the old ones. In our religious rituals, however, this ability is restored through ecstatic trance. Metamorphosis becomes possible once again as trance softens the boundaries between the human world and the world of animals, birds, fish, and plants.

The change in form that is characteristic of metamorphosis was witnessed constantly by the horticulturalists. They saw the cycles of change in their gardens. The seed, which was hard and shriveled, was planted and became a tender green sprout. That sprout grew to become a mature plant, producing blossoms and fruit. Then, in its fullness, that plant was harvested and eaten, to nourish the people. A few of the seeds were saved so that the plant, which had to all appearances died, would be reborn the following planting season.

Metamorphosis postures allow us city dwellers to participate in the changing of form so that we can know what it is to move beyond the boundaries of being human. It is sad that this profound and mystical experience was deplored among the later agricultural religions, Christianity among them. The agriculturalists split themselves from the animal world, considering animals to be unclean and worthy only of serving human interests. Animals, plants, insects, and birds were no longer the teachers and messengers from the powerful forces that guide life on the Earth. They were viewed as primitive, crude, lowly, given to baser instincts, and incapable of communion with God. Today we are paying the price for this disdainful attitude in the form of environmental crises facing the planet. Lacking in respect for the creatures and gifts of the Earth, humans have exploited the natural world for their pleasure and destroyed the balance so precious to the hunter gatherers and horticulturalists.

Now we are faced with the huge task of healing the split between ourselves and the natural world. This split also exists within ourselves, for it is the outcome of a cultural attitude that denounces the animal body, which is also our human body. What we do to our bodies, we do to our souls. I have encountered many sad examples of people trying to live as though their bodies were somehow separate from their selves. For a number of years, I worked as a psychotherapist with women and men who suffered from eating disorders. With painful regularity, they spoke of their disgust for their bodies. They punished their bodies with laxatives and vomiting and starvation in an effort to control the feelings and instincts that were inherent in being aware of themselves physically. Rather than celebrating their natural material bodies, they were afraid of them. I wonder now, looking back on those earlier years as a therapist, if their fears and painful attitudes might have been transformed through trance experiences. They could have joined the Olmec Prince to become huge and magnificent jaguars or gorgeous blue-and-green quetzal birds.

Metamorphosis experiences change us in many ways. By becoming animals, we can no longer stand removed from what happens to animals at the hands of humans. Following is an example from a recent trance I experienced using the Jama-Coaque posture:

> I saw a fox looking at me across a creek [the boundary between ordinary and alternate reality?]. Then I saw an image of a blue fox my uncle had kept in a pen for hunting. "You were kind to that frightened blue fox," said the fox in the woods, "so you may be allowed to have this metamorphosis experience." I suddenly felt very sad and was at the same time furious with men who hunted for sport. I was seeing/being the fox caught in a trap, gnawing my foot off to get free, whimpering. Then I saw foxtail coats and was full of tears and anger.

I had become a fox and could no longer dissociate myself from the realization that fur coats, however beautiful, were the skins of my comrades. If I allowed myself to be open to the foxes' reality, then I could not tolerate the thought of them being hunted for sport or killed mercilessly for the money their pelts would bring. My attitude evolved out of a feeling of kinship rather than out of any effort to be politically correct, and my story is not told in an effort to shame those who wear fur. Our ancestors wore the skins of animals. However, these skins came from animals who gave their bodies as gifts of food to sustain the lives of the people, and our hunter ancestors honored the animals' spirits and were careful to assure that they suffered as little as possible. Because of my metamorphosis experience, I began to believe, as some of my hunter ancestors did, that when we die, we are shown the same compassion or cruelty that we have given our animal brothers and sisters during our lives.

When you experience metamorphosis, you are permitted to become another creature. Nevertheless, your observing ego remains secure throughout the experience, so you have no loss of consciousness or personal identity. In some traditions, this is known as shapeshifting. Shapeshifting is an ability attributed to holy people and sorcerers, and it has always been a puzzle to me, probably since my first reading of Carlos Castaneda's *The Teachings of Don Juan*. How can magicians become crows, or women turn into wolves? There are, of course, many mysteries into which I have not been initiated. Nevertheless, from listening to and participating in many, many metamorphosis trances, I understand one way to make sense of shapeshifting. In trance, people feel their noses extending into snouts, their spines loosening to the suppleness of snakes, their bodies taking on the lumbersome weight of buffalos. And if you, too, are in trance, you can look at these people and see the animal forms, sometimes superimposed over the human shapes. You cross over the line into Alternate Reality and participate in the realm of magic. As Dr. Goodman once explained to me, the power of the shapeshifter may be, in part, the ability to affect others so profoundly that they go into altered states. They cross over the line of ordinary reality and become capable of witnessing the changed form of the shapeshifter in the alternate realm.

The eight metamorphosis postures in this book all have Mesoamerican origins. Several of them—the Bahia, Jama-Coaque, La Tolita, and Machalilla postures—are relatively new to us at the Cuyamungue Institute, having been recently found in a book from Germany: *Ecuador: Gold und Terrakotten*.[28] The Corn Goddess posture is historically the most recent, dating from the time when the Aztecs converted from horticulture to full scale agriculture. This posture offers a weaker metamorphosis, often into some form of plant or insect life. The other postures usually lead you to witness or change into animal forms. The experience of changing into another form requires considerable energy, and if you are new to ecstatic trance, you may need some practice before achieving full metamorphosis. You may just get hot and feel a lot of energy, an indication that you are building up momentum but have not yet attained enough focus and energy to shift fully into metamorphosis. In complete shapeshifting, the presence and experience of a particular animal floods your consciousness.

It is always better to come to the trance experience rested and with an empty stomach. Also, you may have more powerful trances when you do the postures with a group rather than alone. At the Cuyamungue Institute we sometimes have a drumming and rattling session prior to metamorphosis. Everyone plays a percussive instrument and flows into chanting or dancing, all of which raises the energy of the group, sustaining the possibility of a complete shift during the trance.

THE BAHIA POSTURE

    There are numerous cities and villages in Central and South America with the name Bahia, which means "bay." Since the figure in this posture was found among the photographs of Ecuadorian pottery, it was presumed to be from Bahia de Caraquez, or Caraquez Bay, at the mouth of the Chone River on the coast of Ecuador. The figure dates from the period of 300 B.C. to A.D. 800.

The body positioning in this posture is similar to that of the Olmec Prince posture. The distinctive feature of the Bahia posture is the exaggerated extension of the tongue. In many traditions the tongue is extended to enhance the power of contact with the spirit world, since the tongue is a highly sensitized organ, rich with nerve endings. Our very first experience with this posture gave the group of us that had gathered in the kiva an intense and powerful metamorphosis. The saliva dripping from our mouths onto the floor was a little disconcerting, but it was easily cleaned up and everyone agreed that it had not distracted from our shifting into the altered consciousness of trance.

The experience of metamorphosis using the Bahia posture is typical of what you might experience in any of the metamorphosis postures. Judy reported:

> This posture was very, very busy for me. At first my eyesight went black. I was a black leopard walking in the jungle. There was an intense burning in my lungs from running. I then saw a patch of brilliant red flowers. Then I was a striped tiger mother, and there were several babies nursing on me. . . . I then felt myself falling over backward, and my head bumped the kiva wall. I was a frog. I could feel my throat expanding as I sang. I started to jump. It was so much fun I wanted to laugh. I jumped for quite awhile; it was fun. I had a bitter taste in my mouth. Then I saw a drum. I could see the drumstick hit the drum and I could see the sound. I was above a group of drummers, watching all the drumsticks hit the drum and the sound come out.

It is common during metamorphosis to have visceral perceptions. Judy felt burning in her lungs from running. She sensed the tiger cubs nursing at her tits. Her throat expanded into frog "singing," and her body knew how it felt to jump like a frog jumps. She tasted bitterness. At the

end, the effect of the trance on her consciousness was confirmed by her newly found ability to *see* sound.

Pamela described her experience:

> At first it seemed like nothing. Then I asked God to transform me into what He would have me be. I was face to face with a bat—we were about the same size, and he was kind of in a spider's web but not hindered. . . . I became bat, crawled up and around and into a cave and out again. Then I became eagle, with a white head and curly hair, and I was eagle and

woman with a great wing spread, and I seemed to stand with the spread [wings] as eaglewoman. . . . An owl and a crow came. I think I became both briefly and then back to eagle. Then I was standing in a light, and then it was gone. All of this came and went over and over.

Unfortunately, Pamela did not write about the emotional experience of becoming eaglewoman. However, her change in sensations and her expansion into completely new inner perceptions are the hallmark of this wonderous transformation called metamorphosis.

DESCRIPTION

Sit on the floor cross-legged with your right leg on top of your left leg. With your arms stiff and your elbows locked, grasp your right leg with both hands. Your hands should be side by side, about five inches apart, your fingers wrapped around your leg. Keep your thumbs beside your forefingers, not wrapped around the other side of your leg. Open your mouth and complete-ly *extend your tongue so that it is hanging out of your mouth. Close your eyes and look straight ahead.*

THE CHALCHIHUITLIQUE POSTURE

Chalchihuitlique is known as "she who wears a skirt of jade." She is the sister and/or wife of Tlaloc, the Teotihuacan and Aztec god of rain. There are also figures of the Zapotecan rain god Cocijo in this posture. They are primarily found in funerary urns from Monte Alban, Mexico, dating from A.D. 100 to 600.

The story of Chalchihuitlique is told in a myth from Mesoamerica about the cycles of creation:

> In most of the Aztec versions there were four suns, or eras in the past, followed by the present age, that of humanity and historical time, which is known as the Fifth Sun. Each sun was ruled by a separate deity, peopled by different types of humans, and destroyed by a universal cataclysm, in which the people of the age were either completely destroyed or transformed into some other form of life. . . . The Fourth Sun, 4 Atl or Four Water, presided over by Chalchihuitlique, was populated by humans whose food was another kind of wild seed called cencocopi or teocentli, possibly an antecedent of corn, who were victims of a great flood, the survivors of which were transformed into fish.[29]

Some individuals using this posture actually follow this story of a flood in the age of Chalchihuitlique and become fish, either through taking an underwater journey or through experiencing becoming a fish. In her very first trance experience, Susan commented on the unusual visual display: "I was looking up, as if I was in water, like a fish." In the same workshop, Judy said her primary experience was one "of bubbles, like being under water." Neither of them had used this posture before, and they knew nothing about the story of Chalchihuitlique.

Explosions of vibrant colors are common in metamorphosis, presumably because the color expresses the huge surges of energy required to undergo the change of shape in Alternate Reality. Purple, green, blue, black, and gold color people's experiences of shapeshifting. Sometimes equally colorful arrays of animals present themselves in trance. In one trance using the Chalchihuitlique posture, Gwyn saw herself first as a tree growing on the seacoast; then looked out through the eyes of a deer. As the deer, she was shot; as she fell, she turned into a snake. Then she was a rabbit, a skunk, a raccoon, and an owl; she saw a swimming seal, and finally a sea lion, "sitting in sovereignty on a rock."

The continual change of metamorphosis may be only a fluctuation back and forth between opposites. Kathleen said in one trance that she was at times a bat in a cave and at other times a butterfly in a cocoon, both in the dark and observing the color of the outer world. Her perception constantly alternated between the experiences of darkness and the light beyond. Other people go deep into the trance and spend their time in Alternate Reality with only one animal.

Sometimes the Chalchihuitlique trance is not a transformation into an animal form but a learning time with an animal teacher. Carol shared this experience:

> Eagle, who very often takes me into the trance, soared by. The more I do the trances, the more aware I am of Eagle, and his appearances are more "real." My experiences involve more senses and feelings, but I don't know how to verbalize this. This time it was as if Eagle opened his mouth and I saw a man holding a child . . . draped in a white covering . . . and I could see a symbol or drawing on the cloth. The man became Thunderbird and still enfolded the child. There were sun signs on the child's face. Then I saw a clearing in a very dense, bright yellowish-green forest—as in a rain forest. I questioned if [a group of people there] were Mayan or if the symbol on the cloth was Egyptian, and I really wanted to know. Would it help to "know" all that I can before I try the trance so that I could "experience" more? Then I saw the child grow and do things. . . . Then there was a man with an awesome face, as if carved in stone, who was a powerful leader. He also appeared as Sun and Thunderbird. There was a great sun with a teeny hole that the man had to go through to become part of the whole. Then I saw a vagina and a seed pot, and another child emerged: a new cycle.

Carol did not experience a metamorphosis into a different form herself but witnessed the transformation of a human, and perhaps of all humanity, with the help of great Sun and Thunderbird.

DESCRIPTION

Sit on the floor cross-legged, with your left leg in front of your right leg. With your elbows relaxed, place each hand palm down over its corresponding kneecap, so that your right hand is on your right knee and your left hand is on your left knee. Your fingers should extend over your kneecaps in a relaxed fashion. Face directly forward, with your eyes and mouth closed.

THE CORN GODDESS POSTURE

The Aztec Corn Goddess, Cinteotl, was often portrayed as a young woman in this kneeling position. In one story, the first man and first woman had a son who married a goddess. This son and his goddess wife then had a son Centeotl who was buried in the earth. From his body grew plants that became important to human survival—cotton, sweet potatoes, and especially corn.

Corn was so important to the people of Mesoamerica that the Mayan

Popol Vuh tells the story of gods creating humans from corn. In one of my early trances with the Corn Goddess posture, I was a participant in just such a creation, or re-creation:

> I am first broken down into molecules and then reshaped. Someone is chewing corn, breaking down the starch, changing its composition. With the chewed corn they are shaping me, making me into my new form. Now I will be a "made" person.

In the Tewa tradition, among the Pueblo Indians along the northern Rio Grande, Made People are those who are initiated into one of the religious societies.[30] I experienced a transformation that helped me understand what it might mean to be "made." I felt a kinship with the Corn Goddess, being made of her body.

A few years ago, the U.S. Post Office issued an airmail stamp showing the wooden carving of a catlike figure in this posture. The carving was discovered in a peat bog on Key Marco, Florida, and was made by the Calusa people A.D. 700 to 1450. It was a slight variation of the Aztec posture, as the hands were drawn closer together on the thighs, and the shoulders were hunched.

The Aztecs converted from small-garden horticulture to agriculture, in which they cleared and planted large fields of crops. That change in lifestyle affected the way these people related to the beings who inhabited the alternate, spiritual reality. Metamorphosis as the key religious experience waned. The effects of this change are felt when this posture is used for metamorphosis trance. The experience is less potently focused on becoming an animal. In this posture, people are more likely to become insects or plant forms. Sometimes they describe the sensation of breaking through the ground and growing, or of being part of a field full of blossoms.

Despite the fact that this posture comes from a time when horticulture was waning, those who have used it have learned a great deal from the Corn Goddess. In this posture, more than any other, people have experienced feeling a rearranging of their molecules, letting go of the accustomed structure of self. Shapeshifting is not just a change into another form but a shift into a reconstructed mode of witnessing and being in the world. Brief episodes of being without the usual sense of self, of having a different essential focus, are profound. It is in these situations that the beauty of the ritual postures is most pronounced.

Western psychiatry tells us that to be without the boundaries that define the self can be devastating; it is what we know as psychotic. In trance, however, we are both in this world and in the other realms at the same time. In ordinary reality, I may kneel on the floor of my room with my observing ego intact, while in the other reality I may perceive myself being reorganized at a molecular level, transfigured into another being. I experience deep empathy with the other, whether it is a butterfly or a bear or a corn plant. I share the other's way of being in the world for a brief while, yet I never lose my anchor in myself, which is *my* vehicle for being in the world in this life.

This sense of sharing in the realities of other beings was reflected in the following Corn Goddess trance experienced by Pamela:

> I saw my medicine bowl, oval shaped and rough wood. . . . Then I was looking through the top of one corn plant, very close up. I saw a whole cornfield, beautiful, and a blue sky with white puffy clouds, and the cornfield sprouted corn on the cob like a fountain (felt like abundance). Then Eagle appeared and . . . I became Eagle and flew over the field. Then I became Hawk and flew. Then I was a little mouse at the base of the corn plant. Then I was me, and my bowl was there in the cornfield and it had corn kernels in it. Eagle picked up Mouse and I was afraid [he] would kill it but [he] flew to a high peak and returned. I served Eagle, Hawk, and Mouse corn kernels from the bowl, kneeling in the field, and then animal

after animal came in a column and I served each one. They came from the forest and went through the field over a hill. . . . Finally Bear came and I served, and Bear served me and returned the bowl. I followed Bear to the edge of the hill with Mouse and waved goodbye. Mouse and I were joyous and danced in the field. . . . I put Mouse down and he scurried away.

DESCRIPTION
Assume a kneeling positon, with your legs parallel and touching each other. Your knees should be bent so that your buttocks rest on your heels. If

you have a knee problem, you can use a pillow on your heels for support. Place your hands palm down on top of your upper thighs, positioned so that the heels of your hands are just at the crease where your thigh joins your torso. Hold your fingers close together, and point toward your knees. Your shoulders are stiff and slightly raised, and your arms are close to your body. Face directly ahead, with your eyes closed.

THE JAMA-COAQUE POSTURE

This posture comes from the elaborately decorated figure that is the cover piece for the German book *Ecuador: Gold und Terrakotten.* The figure is wearing a heavy necklace with three strands and a medallion hung from it; he also wears earlobe plugs, a nose decoration, and an attachment that protrudes from his chin. His posture is similar to the Machalilla and Man of Cuautla postures.

Jama is a small market center on the north central coast of Ecuador. The word Coaque refers to a culture that flourished there a few centuries ago, but there is no specific information about that group of people.

This is not an easy position to maintain for fifteen minutes. The spirits can and do help. Robinette reported as part of her trance, "[I was shown] a way to get in the posture so it wasn't difficult for me." As my colleagues and I have experimented with unknown postures, we have had to rely on this type of aid from Alternate Reality. Sometimes carved figures twist their extremities into impossible angles; one Mexican urn is shaped in the Feathered Serpent posture, with the little man sitting back on huge buttocks that support him in a way no human form imaginably could. Because of the peculiarities of a posture, it can be painful. At the beginning of performing a Jama-Coaque posture, Kathleen reported, "I thought I would faint," but further into trance her body began to move rhythmically and she noted, "I was no longer aware of my legs hurting." Her experience was one of an odd sense of movement, unlike anything she felt consciously able to initiate. She concluded with a comment that she had perhaps learned how it felt to be a particular animal, but unfortunately the animal had not made itself known to her.

The building of energy that is typical of metamorphosis trances is experienced in this posture. One workshop participant spoke of feeling as though she was swirling in a vortex. Another said that "the trance started with an intense swirling in my head, so much so that my head wanted to fall backwards. . . . I was very dizzy."

Judy described a trance that was characteristic of those experienced by people using the Jama-Coaque posture. She saw and felt the jungle, and at one point may have become a monkey, but the trance was not strong enough for a full metamorphosis.

> I was in a jungle. I heard a loud bird call, and beneath the rattle were
> bird sounds throughout the trance. A very stylized bird masked-dancer

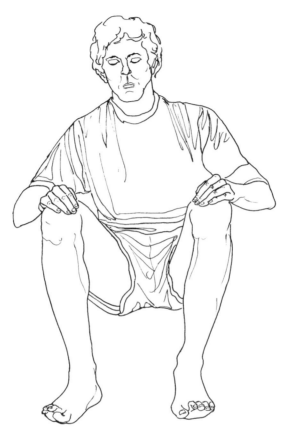

came. . . . He took my hands and we moved in a circle. . . . The masked dancer and I started off through the jungle. . . . I think I may have been a monkey. The trees in the jungle were very close together, and I could barely see masks peering through the trees. I then saw snakes winding up these trees. At the very end we were in a clearing, searching through this pile of sand. We were looking for jewels, and I found a green one and a diamond-like one.

It will be important for Judy to explore the meaning of finding jewels at the end of her trance experience, using the techniques of amplification and association learned during divination trances.

This is a relatively new posture for those of us at the Cuyamungue Institute, and our experiences with it have not been the clear transformations into animals that we associate with other metamorphosis postures. It is possible that the ritual uses of the posture were deteriorating in Ecuador when the figure was made, so the power of the trance is less intense. It is also possible that this pose mediates visceral experiences that are transformative but may be less related to animal forms. Gwyn shared this trance:

> We are searching for a golden treasure. It is as though we are descending deep into the shaft of a gold mine. Someone is walking up ahead with a torch or flashlight held high in front of him. I have a sensation in my body of being connected with the body of the Earth and of knowing a very deep and profound ancient wisdom. It is as though the posture mediates an electromagnetic resonance between the Earth's core vibration and my own physiological electromagnetic quality.

Although she did not shapeshift, the trance was metamorphic for Gwyn, changing her physically and offering the expansion of awareness that is so characteristic of metamorphosis postures.

DESCRIPTION

Sit on the floor with your legs stretched out in front of you, about twelve inches apart. Bend your knees and draw your feet closer to your body. Place only the heel of each foot on the floor, so that your feet are at right angles to your lower legs. Place your right hand palm down over your right knee. Cup your left hand with the fingertips bunched together and rest only the fingertips on your left knee. Relax your arms and hold them close to your body. Keep your spine straight. Face forward, with your tongue protruding slightly from between your lips.

THE LA TOLITA POSTURE

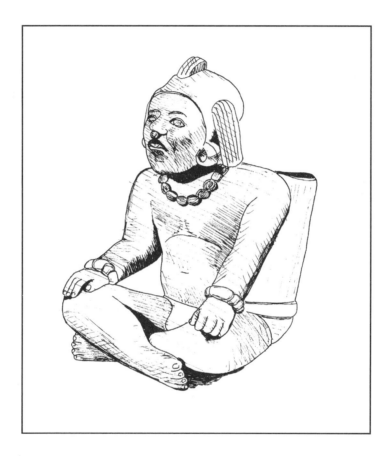

This posture comes from a red-glazed ceramic figure with a winsome face that was found in the same German publication of Ecuadorian pottery as the Jama-Coaque posture. The reference in the book says simply that it is from La Tolita-Kultur, dating from 300 B.C. to A.D. 800. Today the island of La Tolita is located at the northern end of the coast of Ecuador. The feminine form of the name refers to the island, not the gender of the clay figure, which is quite clearly male. The little man looked at first as though he were sitting in the Chalchihuitlique posture, but the stiffness of his left arm, his slouch, and his upturned face revealed differences that were later clear in the trance itself. Dressed in only a loincloth, the figure is nevertheless well decorated, with bracelets on each arm, a necklace, and plugs in his earlobes and nose. He wears an unusual cap, with earflaps that look like small wings and another similar flap rising from the top of his head. Our group at the Cuyamungue Institute has yet to replicate the cap, and we cannot say whether it is just an adornment or whether it plays an active part in producing a distinctive trance.

People comment with great regularity on what pleasant, enjoyable experiences they have in the La Tolita posture. In one workshop, a man remarked that the posture was so relaxing he dozed off, and the woman sitting next to him agreed that she was so comfortable she could have stayed in the trance a long, long time.

In that same workshop, the first few people said they had little or no visual experience, only displays of yellow across otherwise blank screens. Then someone saw an old-fashioned biplane. Another became aware of looking out through slits of eyes and seeing everything very close and blurry. Later, piecing together a series of fragments, these four people discovered that they had shared a metamorphosis into dragonflies. Even though such joint trance experiences happen often, still they are remarkable. People seated together in a workshop, or across the room from each other, can share similar experiences, as though they have unconsciously agreed to join hands and wander into the same corner of the other realm in trance.

In that group, four people were transformed into snakes, three became frogs, four became eagles, and two became wildcats. Another knew only that her shoulders had become massive and her legs huge as she transformed into an unknown being. In another, smaller group, two women had the experience of being a butterfly, although Marianne was a caterpillar molting just before its metamorphosis into a butterfly, while Sherry said, "I was the body of a huge butterfly slowly spreading my massive wings."

The purpose of metamorphosis is not to tranform into some predetermined form, although societies that revered a particular animal may have used a posture specifically to join with that animal in Alternate Reality. What is more important for workshop participants I have known is the shift of attitude that results from being the other. Sara spoke of being a cobra. "People only saw the ferociousness," she said, but she experienced the coolness at the center of the cobra. She discovered that its power came not from its poison, but from its cool calm center.

At other times, an animal spirit becomes a direct teacher. Sandra became an eagle and was soaring in the sky when a rock or shot hit her. As she started to plummet, the eagle flying with her came to her side, assuring her, "You'll be okay," and showing her how to catch the wind to rise to a higher level. In trance she had the physical experience of dropping, dropping, and then finding the current and letting it lift her up again. She found that the words of a friend were a support when life knocked her down. Now her body remembers how to find the currents and fly again after a blow. She can draw on this strength in her ordinary life when she is faced with challenges.

Sometimes the lessons are intended to correct a faulty or offensive attitude. Recently in La Tolita posture, I was in a jungle and saw macaws flying above the trees. I wanted to "be a macaw" and tried to maneuver myself into transforming into one of these gorgeous birds by imagining what it might be like to fly with them. I was immediately met by the presence, although not the vision, of the old macaw grandfathers. They were angry with the impertinence of my barging into their realm, without invitation or preparation. It was only because I had made a parrot mask at the Trance Dance a few years ago, they said, that I had gained entrance to their world at all. If I came with more humility, asking rather than demanding, they would teach me. The rattling ended and I had learned my lesson.

The power of the La Tolita posture was reflected in an experience of

a woman who had been working with the ritual body postures for many years. During her first trance with this posture, she went through an initiation. At the end, she commented:

> This was definitely a metamorphosis posture, only, for me, it was a change that took place on a very, very deep level. The buildings kept changing as I walked that fine line between the realities. I did not change into something that I was not; I changed into that which I truly am!

DESCRIPTION

Sit cross-legged on the floor, with your right leg in front of your left leg. Rest your right hand palm down on your right knee, and hold your arm away from your body. Hold your left arm rigid, with your elbow locked. Curl your left hand into a fist and rest it on your left knee. Slouch forward slightly, but hold your head up, facing forward. Rest your tongue between your lips.

THE MACHALILLA POSTURE

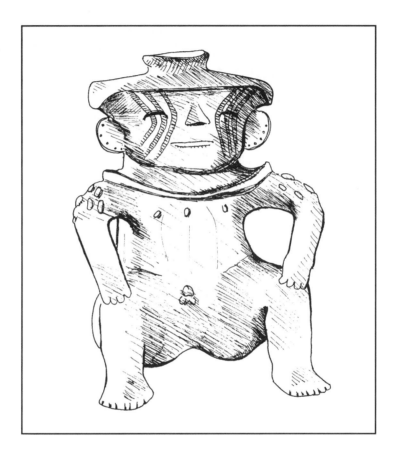

    Machalilla is a village of the Manabi province in the forested lowlands of western Ecuador. This posture is from a ceramic urn depicting a man sitting on his haunches with his legs spread open. The urn dates from 1500 to 1200 B.C., an earlier period than that of the other metamorphosis postures of that area. A similar terracotta figure was found in a gravesite in the Jalisco province of Mexico, dating from 200 B.C. to A.D. 200.

The energy required for and available from trance is clearly experienced by those using the Machalilla posture, as well as the other metamorphosis postures. One person's body trembled and began swaying; she experienced the sudden presence of a very bright light and a slight feeling of nausea accompanying the burst of energy. Pamela saw a snake that moved faster and faster until it transformed into a hawk and soared. In my own recent trance with this posture, I realized that I had forgotten to stick out my tongue. When I did, there was an immediate rush of light and power that was too much; it overwhelmed me and threw me out of focus. In another trance, I was observing a colt frolicking in a pasture. Then, without warning, energy burst through the horse's skin and I saw only a being of white light in the form of a horse.

A characteristic of trances mediated by the Machalilla posture is a significant change in perspective. One woman described moving between the realms of ordinary and nonordinary realities. She saw the Rain Serpent, the Avanyu of the American Southwest, gliding over the tops of the mountains, looking over the land with a benign but distant gaze. The Rain Serpent was available to the Earth and her creatures, but was removed from them, part of another realm. The woman recognized how insignificant the daily turmoil of her own life appeared from the Rain Serpent's point of view; it was not that the events of her life were unimportant, only that they were not so world-shattering as they seemed when she was caught up in the middle of them.

Following is Robinette's trance experience, which makes the point clearly:

> I experienced a change in perspective physically, literally seeing my life
> from different angles. At one point I was a dolphin, diving backward,
> [aware of] the ease and smoothness of the water, and I saw the tiny key near
> Key West. Then I was a big crow turning my neck to look at my back.
> Heard: "When you look at your shadow you must look at that which every

one else can see [your back], but you never do." Saw the past in a new way, saw it through various people's eyes. Crawled between my legs from behind and saw my life from that perspective. Heard: "Metamorphosis is not just shapeshifting, it is a shift in self concept, perception, perspective."

This is a difficult posture to maintain and many people find it too uncomfortable. One person reported, "This posture was extremely uncomfortable for me. I got very, very hot. I had a splitting headache on the right half of my face and eye. I had to bring my tongue in to relieve the pressure. I also felt nauseated." In all ritual body postures, and especially with extremely powerful ones, it is crucial to maintain the exact position. It is likely that this person shifted out of the proper position and as a result felt discomfort and nausea.

DESCRIPTION

Sit on the floor with your legs as wide apart as possible, your knees bent and your legs drawn up toward your body. Your feet should be sole down on the floor. Arch your arms away from your body. With your right hand at your right knee and your left hand at your left knee, form the fingertips of each hand into a circle around their respective kneecaps. It is as if you grasp each kneecap with your fingertips and gently tug on it. Rest your tongue between your lips as you face forward, your eyes closed.

THE OLMEC PRINCE POSTURE

    Archaeologists named the figure from which this posture was obtained the Prince because of its unusual ornate headdress. It was found in the Mexican state of Tabasco, and dates from 1100 to 600 B.C. During this time, the Olmecs developed a sophisticated society in Central America. As they were horticultural in their social organization, their ultimate spiritual experience would have been metamorphosis. Among the

Olmecs, the jaguar was the most important of the animal spirits in Alternate Reality. It is not surprising, then, that people commonly transform into the magnificent being of the jaguar during metamorphosis trance using the Olmec Prince posture.

My first experience with the Olmec Prince posture was in 1984 when I visited New Mexico and the Cuyamungue Institute for the first time. As I was from Ohio, I was unaccustomed to the altitude, which is about 7000 feet at the Cuyamungue Institute, fifteen miles north of Santa Fe. Even more staggering to me, however, was the immensity of the sky and mountains stretching out for miles around us. Out in the mountain desert, in what the locals call the Pojoaque Badlands, we climbed a road up to the ridge every morning and evening at sunrise and sunset—to greet the morning light and to give thanks for the day that was ending. It seemed like I could see forever. The Sangre de Cristo Mountains, turned crimson by the setting sun, were magnificent; and without benefit of trance or posture, I was already transformed.

My journal entry from this first trance with the Olmec Prince contained several elements typical of metamorphosis:

> I feel like a big cat walking through a jungle forest, then sitting on a rocky ledge overlooking the jungle. It becomes night and I am prowling, hunting. I pounce on a small animal, killing it for my food. I approach a village where there is a bonfire. An African man is performing some kind of ceremony. In the flames of the bonfire I see the face of a tiger. The scene changes. Kizzie [the German Shepherd who lived at the Cuyamungue Institute] turns into a wolf with a baby in its mouth, then back to Kizzie with a stick in her mouth, then back to the wolf, and I become the wolf to walk through the hills. [There is an] image of geometrical design, then vivid color and intense light just beyond my reach. I ask how I can get there and voice says, "Come slowly." Then [there is] a golden bee and the experience of swarming in a hive.

Without knowing anything about the posture, I went immediately into metamorphosis as a member of the large cat family. Just being at the Cuyamungue Institute and going into trance several times a day had, I believe, prepared me to shift easily into ecstatic trance, without requiring the usual buildup of energy. I saw the cat's home environment, so much different from the desert in which I was living at the time, and experienced the feeling of killing for food. The power of the trance waned for a while as I witnessed Kizzie changing back and forth into a wolf. Then there was a final rally as abstract geometrical designs burst with color and light. With the final surge of energy, I was invited to continue my journey toward the light beyond my reach, but I was advised to come slowly. The bee reminded me of the magnificent process of metamorphosis into which I was initiated as the rattling ended.

The image of the wolf with the baby in its mouth was connected for me with an illustrated book of Grimms' fairytales from my childhood. At an early age I was influenced by my culture; I learned to view the wolf, once revered as a powerful spiritual figure, as the Big Bad Wolf with snapping jaws who stole babies from their cradles if mothers were negligent. In the trance, however, I became the wolf to rediscover her wild beauty. A German shepherd escorted me across the barrier of my culture to the forest home of the wolf, who has since become a special friend and teacher.

Many, many workshop participants report with wonder on their very real impressions of hunting, killing, eating, bathing, and mating as animals. The taste of blood in the mouth or the ripple of huge muscles carrying a heavy and powerful body are extensions of consciousness that bring people en rapport with wildness.

Metamorphosis with the Olmec Prince is not always a transformation into a cat or even a mammal. Once I found that I became a whale. I wrote in my journal of "not using eyes as the primary means of experiencing. No hands and arms for interacting with the environment; not intellect, reason, or insight as I am accustomed to using, but a deeper

wisdom." It was so foreign to my idea of being in the world to realize that "they [the whales] don't hunt or make nests or homes." Instead I embraced the pleasure of long ocean journeys and felt tones, "rich and varied, as beautiful as landscapes."

In my first Olmec Prince trance, the presence of an African man and a tiger suggested that it did not take place in Central America. Sometimes the figure of a posture leads the person in trance to its homeland, but that is by no means always the case. Judith once saw, in an Olmec Prince trance, an enormous black panther in an Egyptian pose. Even though it was very still and had crystals for claws and teeth, it was alive. A door opened in its stomach, inviting her into a long and marvelous journey, and when she returned she was marked on her forehead by the panther. So, while metamorphosis allows you to share in an animal's ordinary reality, you are sometimes taken into nonordinary experiences as well.

DESCRIPTION

Sit on the floor with your right leg crossed in front of your left leg. Stretch your arms straight in front of your body with your elbows locked, and bring your hands down to the floor in front of your legs. Curl each hand so that only the middle segment of each finger actually rests on the floor. Make sure your knuckles, wrists, elbows, and shoulders are rigid.

You may lean forward; however, be sure to keep your back straight and to move forward from your hip joints. Lean your head forward slightly, with your eyes looking straight ahead, but closed. Protrude your tongue from between your lips.

The clay figure in this posture wears a headdress and earrings. These accoutrements have not been duplicated, so their effects on the trance are not documented.

Variation: *Assume the same sitting position. However, rather than resting your hands on the floor, use them to grasp your right leg. Your tongue does not protrude from your lips, and your head is thrown back as far as possible.*

THE TATTOOED JAGUAR POSTURE

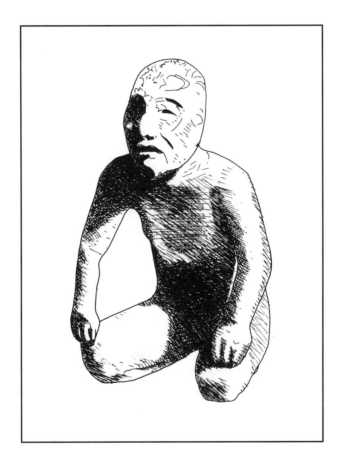

The figure of the Tattooed Jaguar from which this posture is taken is in a book about the Olmecs, the horticulturalists who lived in what is today Mexico and Guatemala.[31] It is dated between 1400 and 400 B.C. On one page of the book is a pottery sculpture of a kneeling man whose head bears the tattoos that characterize this posture. Several pages later, in text that is unrelated to the earlier figure, is another figure in the same kneeling pose but whose head is a jaguar mask bearing the same tattoos. These two figures beautifully illustrate what occurs in the trance. The person begins the trance as a human and becomes a jaguar but never loses the human connection through his or her body, which remains in the ritual posture.

Following is an example of a Tattooed Jaguar trance from my own experiences:

> It is night. The lush darkness is full of voluptuous odors. Briefly [there is] an image of the jaguar trotting along through an open space, then, as a flash in a mirror, the gold glint of eyes in a face shadowed by the play of leaves on a bright, hot afternoon. There is the taste of blood in my mouth, and as my tongue rolls around I feel sharp powerful teeth, and I remember them sinking deep into flesh. I am running, and all of my being is in this strong supple body that runs through the night, deeply satisfied to be what I am. No thought, just the sensual pleasure of being in this body.

What a privilege to have the doors of this beautiful animal's perception opened to us. There are skeptics who question whether we can really know how an animal perceives—whether the pleasures and pain we experience in metamorphosis have any connection with an animal's true awareness. Of course, there is no way to verify the similarity of trance with a jaguar's experience. However, what we can know is that metamorphosis changes how we experience ourselves, stretching the limits of our own consciousness and often releasing us from the limits imposed by the "civilization" of our urban culture. Jan Price, a psychotherapist well-seasoned in ecstatic trance, described metamorphosis as the ultimate empathy needed for ultimate healing. Without the benefit of being able to shift into alternative perspectives of ourselves, we are unable to sense the imbalances in ourselves, in the other species that share the planet with us, and in the Earth herself.

In doing this trance, many individuals become sensitized to the non-human world and grow in rapport with the animals. Thus, they feel a sense of wounds being healed. This can be a healing of torn energy patterns or changes in the physical body. In her first experience with the Tattooed Jaguar, Judi was so moved by her heightened awareness that she spent the last part of her trance "making amends to all the plants and animals I have harmed." For her, the healing involved her relationships with the natural world. In the same workshop, Deborah experienced a healing: "[The huge cat] worked on my throat, then killed me as prey and wore me on its back." In what might have seemed like a terrible ordeal, she released the shoulder tension she had held persistently for years.

Perhaps understandably, not everyone is ready to embrace all that metamorphosis offers. One man sensed that a kill scene was imminent and rejected it. Another described the fear of "having forces around that I'm not in control of." Elizabeth very beautifully acknowledged that she had to dive into what was happening to her or die: "In order to know, sometimes we have to be wounded and killed, to feel the fear." Then we can come face to face with the power, beauty, and strength of a jaguar and ourselves.

DESCRIPTION

Kneel on the floor with your knees spread so that your thighs form a "V". You may find it comfortable to cross your right big toe over your left big toe, as Japanese men do when assuming their traditional kneeling position. Bend your knees so that your buttocks rest on your heels. If this is impossible, place a pillow under your buttocks and thighs for support. Bend forward slightly at your waist. Curl your hands the amount that would be required to hold a medium-sized candle. Place your curled left hand palm-side down on your left knee. Place your right hand on your right knee, tilted so that a candle held in that hand would be at 45-degree angle from your knee. Keep your elbows relaxed, and slightly bow your arms. Face directly forward, with your eyes closed.

Spirit Journeys

Imagine what it was like back in the days when all humans were hunter gatherers. There were no telephones or radios for communication, no systems like radar to predict the weather, no cars or trains or airplanes for transportation, no television or films or libraries for entertainment. Elizabeth Marshall Thomas, in her novel *Reindeer Moon,*[32] wonderfully described what that world might have been like. The shamans in those early societies were highly sophisticated in their abilities to make journeys into the spirit world. They were able to communicate over long distances in trance, as evidenced in the stories of skilled medicine people who visited their counterparts in other areas of the world. They could interact with the winds and the thunder beings and the cloud people to know about the weather. They could journey in trance as far as the moon and the other planets in our solar system, as verified by the Old Ones who told of the moons of Jupiter before modern space travel brought news of their existence. And what better entertainment during the long darkness of winter than to travel in the sky nations or hear the stories the animal spirits could tell?

In the Harner method, the act of undertaking any shamanic trance is called journeying. This is not surprising given that the training Michael Harner received from his teacher in eastern Peru seems to have been based on the hunter-gatherer tradition. The hunter gatherers were the people who perfected spirit journeying. The posture Harner was taught, and which is recommended for going to the spirit world, is a spirit-journey posture referred to in this book as the South American Lower World posture. While it is true that every posture involves a transition of "journey" from ordinary to nonordinary reality, those of us who work with ritual body postures do not use the term "journeying" to describe every ecstatic trance. We save that term only for the postures that take us on journeys through the three realms of the Lower World, the Middle World, and the Upper World.

In a spirit journey, you travel along the Tree of the World. This tree stands in the center of the universe. When you travel into its deep and winding roots, you are in the Lower World. This Lower World is not Hell as defined by the agricultural religious traditions such as Christianity, but is instead the home of the animal spirits; also within the Lower World is the Realm of the Dead.

The Middle World, which is the trunk of the Tree of the World, is the spirit counterpart to the world in which we live. Black Elk spoke of the world "where there is nothing but the spirits of all things. That is the real world that is behind this one, and everything we see here is something like a shadow from that world."[33] In the Middle World exist the spirits that are the essence of everything we know in the material realm, giving vitality to all things that are in form.

One year around Christmastime I was making a spirit journey, and at the very beginning of the trance I saw my chest open and a Christmas tree revealed. Afterward, when I was describing the trance, I noticed the Christmas tree painted on my sweatshirt. I realized that I had seen its spirit counterpart in trance, probably because it represents the Tree of the World in my culture. The Middle World is so truly parallel to this world of ordinary reality that when we journey across it at the time of death, as in the Priestess of Malta posture, we can visit all the places and people and things we have loved in this life for one last time.

The upper branches of the Tree of the World compose the Sky World, the Star Nations, the home of those spirits who exist beyond Earth but who nevertheless interact with us. It is in this Upper World that the original patterns, which are the blueprints for all things, exist. Dr. Goodman wrote: "One of the most pervasive traditions of shamanic culture is the insight that there exists a patterned cosmological order, which can be disturbed by human activity."[34] The gathering hunters knew of this order and generally maintained harmony with the Upper World by behaving appropriately in daily living and by using rituals. When the balance between the human world and the original pattern was disturbed, it was possible to make a spirit journey to the Upper World to make things right again. There is a Zuni story of a young hunter who repeatedly failed to carry out the necessary rituals when he killed animals. He had to make a journey to the Sun and undertake a series of tasks to make right what he had disturbed through his inattention to the rituals that sustained the order between the worlds.

People can carry information to the Great Ones whose task it is to oversee human life on this planet. In the first trance experience using the Venus of Galgenberg posture, a group of us were part of this process. Jan was taken into a "very complex multidimensional matrix," an "extremely complicated pattern," where she traveled along lines and then between spaces.[35] She learned in the trance that making a sound helped to "make shifts or turns or connections between the parts of the matrix that hadn't been connected before." Her comment afterward was, "(T)his seemed to be the obverse of divination; I was taking information up there and then was called on to rearrange the patterns."

A comparison can be made between metamorphosis and spirit journeys. In metamorphosis, you soften your boundaries and expand your experience by being the other; in spirit journeys, you expand your experience by being "there"—by going to the other place that lies beyond the limited world you have known without benefit of an altered state of consciousness. Such a journey can be recreational, just as you might visit an unknown and perhaps exotic place on a vacation. It is always instructive, making your view of the universe and the context of your life larger.

On journeys in which I travel beyond the Earth, into the darkness of space toward other places that also seem like home to me, I look back at our little green planet and feel a wave of tenderness. At those times Gaia, the consciousness of the planet, glows. From the distance, I see her struggles and her strength, and I am happy that I am a part of her. I return to the Earth awakened. As ecopsychologist Theodore Roszak would put it, I return with an "ecological ego mature(d) toward a sense of ethical responsibility with the planet that is as vividly experienced as our ethical responsibility to other people." It is the goal of ecopsychology to "awaken the inherent sense of environmental reciprocity that lies within the ecological unconscious . . . to heal the . . . fundamental alienation between the person and the natural environment."[36] Imagine what changes might occur if hundreds of thousands of people began to journey beyond the boundaries of the urban industrial world, into the Sky World or the Lower World, into the spirit world that is interwoven with our daily living. Perhaps there we might be aroused to our "ecological unconscious" and find a pathway to sanity instead of self-destruction.

The ritual body postures used for journeying to the Sky World are the Lascaux Cave posture and the Venus of Galgenberg posture. The Long Man of Wilmington posture facilitates communication with the Sky World, but experience suggests that some people may not journey as far with this posture as with the other two. In the Priestess of Malta posture, you can travel over the Middle World, seeing the spirit counterparts of daily life; this posture was probably used by shamanesses whose task it was to accompany the soul of one who had just died as it traveled around the world in preparation for leaving this plane of existence. The Albatross posture seems more for journeying into the seas and oceans of the spirit world. The Sami Lower World posture and the South American Lower World posture are used just as their names would suggest—for trips into the Lower World. Also in the Lower World is the place where the spirits of the dead live, and you can go there—at least to the edge of this realm—using the posture known as the Trip to Realm of the Dead.

ALBATROSS POSTURE

The marble figures of a man and a woman from which this posture was obtained were found together in an Etowah gravesite in Bartow County, Georgia. They are about two feet tall, and there is clearly evidence of their having been painted. As is usually the case, there is no indication of the nature of the trance experiences mediated by the male and female versions of this posture, but the greenish-blue masks painted on the upper face of each figure and the open mouths and protruding tongues are clues that both versions of the posture were used for ritual purposes. The Bartow County pair date from approximately A.D. 700. A figure of the female version was also found in Kentucky, but no male counterpart was discovered at that site. The male figure's posture is simi-

lar to the Chalchihuitlique posture, except that his teeth are showing and his tongue is protruding. The people who lived in the southeastern United States were relatives of the Maya and the Aztecs, and there could certainly be a connection between the Albatross posture and those discovered along the Gulf of Mexico.

The name for this posture, the Albatross, came from the reports of several participants from the first group to experiment with it. Subsequent experiences have affirmed that journeying into and over water is typical of this posture's trance. For example, one person described being

in "a little white boat on a green sea, bobbing around under the hot sun." Another told of a gray sea with no boat, and of just being part of the water. The same grayness pervaded another woman's trance, but the cold dark water was inviting. Judy experienced fluidity, and the currents of water as the "winds of the sea." She was also told to "eat fish."

This posture's trance is usually saturated with energy, which propels men rapidly forward into the Middle World and causes women to fly with the birds and the winds. Men and women alike describe feeling nausea, intensity, and sometimes severe heat and pain; sometimes they have to return to their bodies because the out-of-body sensations are too uncomfortable. Spirit journeying can be strenuous on nervous systems unaccustomed to the intensity of it. Our hunter-gatherer ancestors were certainly in better shape physically than we are because of their rigorous lifestyle. When trance results in sensations of nausea, dizziness, or weakness, it is best to eat lightly the day of the trance, but after the trance to eat something to bring blood sugar levels back to normal. It is also helpful to practice with postures that mediate gentler trances, and to check the body's position in the trance to assure that each characteristic gesture and placement is exact.

Men using the male version of the Albatross posture seem to have trance experiences that mimic sexual activity, which is often pronounced in spirit-journey trances. They report exaggerated movements and repeated penetration, along with the experience of traveling at a very high speed. Women, on the other hand, seem more directly attuned to the Sky World, if they are not in the sea.

One of my early experiences with this posture took place in the kiva at the Cuyamungue Institute. A Masked Trance Dance had already taken place the week before, and only a few of us remained on the land. It was painfully dry and we needed rain desperately. We worried about the garden and the desert wildlife, knowing that all were suffering from the drought. I had never gone into trance using this posture and did not

know what to expect. When the rattling began, I saw a small boat in the sea; then the top part of my body flew away. For a while there were no images, but I was very hot and experienced intense but unfocused awareness. Then I saw Dr. Goodman standing on a ridge twirling what appeared to be a bullroarer. She was young and wearing a feather breastpiece and headdress. Somehow I knew she was calling the Sky Beings.

I felt the response of immense and powerful beings. They asked me why I had called them. I felt as though I had telephoned the president of the United States and had him on the line, waiting, ready to respond to the purpose of my call. After a frozen moment or two, when my mind didn't function at all, I told them I was just learning to use this posture, but since they had come, could they please bring rain? "What will you sacrifice?" they asked. "What do you want?" I replied. "Chew some corn

meal and place it on the altar in the kiva," was their instruction. The trance ended with Eagle ripping me open with a huge white talon and pulling something out of me. Then I became Eagle and we flew out into the essence.

With my face still painted blue from the trance (replicating the blue mask painted on the upper face of the figures in this posture), I went into the wooden building where we had our kitchen. I pulled down one of the big metal bins where we stored the grains and flour to keep them from being eaten by the desert mice, and took out a handful of blue cornmeal. Chewing dry cornmeal is no simple task. Slowly I chewed, making more and more saliva, mixing it with the meal in my mouth. Finally it was a mush. I entered the kiva alone to leave my little gift on the altar we had created at the center of the kiva during the Masked Dance. As I did this,

I recalled the Mayan myth in the *Popol Vuh* about the gods making people out of cornmeal. The corn gave its body and I gave the moisture in my mouth to form a gift for the spirits.

As I stepped outside the kiva door and made my way up the hill, I realized that there were sprinkles of rain on my face. It was only a few drops, but even that was more moisture than we had had for several weeks. I smiled, believing the spirits had heard my request and received my gift— and that they had responded. My spirit journey was not just the product of my imagination. The rain on my face proved to me that what we do is real if we are willing to allow it to be so.

DESCRIPTION

Female version: *Sit in a kneeling position with your knees slightly apart and your buttocks resting on your heels. Using a pillow on your heels does not interfere with the trance and is a help if you are otherwise unable to kneel for fifteen minutes. Place your hands palm down against your upper thighs, just below the hip joints, to the sides of your body. Hold your fingers close together and point them toward your knees; relax your thumbs so they are held close to your fingers. Bending from your hips and keeping your spine straight, lean forward slightly. Allow your tongue to rest on your lower teeth and protrude from your lips. Look straight ahead.*

The original figures of these postures both wear a greenish-blue mask. The female figure's mask covers her forehead, nose, and upper cheekbones. The lower edge of the mask and the eyeholes are outlined in black. You can use face paint to duplicate the mask.

Male version: *Sit cross-legged, tailor fashion, keeping your torso straight. Cup your hands over your knees. Place your left leg in front of your right leg and your right leg on top of, rather than behind, your left one. Allow your tongue to protrude from between your lips without tensing your tongue.*

The painted mask on the male figure's face is similar to the one on the female's face, but it extends farther down his face, to just below his cheekbones.

THE LASCAUX CAVE POSTURE

In 1940 a huge cave was discovered near the French village of Montignac. Inside, on the massive walls of the cave, were drawings made from a mixture of charcoal and tallow, dating from 15,000 B.C. These Lascaux Cave drawings gave modern people a glimpse into the richly complex and sophisticated spiritual life of people who had been collectively considered primitives. A ritual body posture identified among the cave drawings was depicted as a stick figure of a man lying in front of a giant aurochs. Various archaeologists speculated that either he had been killed by the aurochs or the drawing related to some kind of hunting magic.

From the perspective of ecstatic trance, neither of these explanations is correct. First, the man is not dead because he quite clearly has an erection, a condition obviously impossible for a corpse. Second, the man's head is a bird mask, and beside him stands a staff with a bird at its head. These suggest that the man is a shaman, journeying as a bird into the Sky World, perhaps with the assistance of a bird who is his spirit helper.

This was the first spirit-journey posture identified by Dr. Goodman, and it was a credit to her skills in observation that she noticed that the body of the shaman was not lying flat. It was, instead, lying at a 37-degree angle. This very precise angle was a hallmark of spirit-journey postures performed by hunters, especially for journeying to the Sky World. For example, this same posture turned up twelve thousand years later in Egypt, in a drawing of Osiris. Osiris underwent a typical shamanic initiation in which his body was dismembered and then reassembled by his sister before he made his spirit journey to the Upper World. In the drawing, Osiris was lying at the same 37-degree angle as the shaman in the Lascaux cave. The only variations in the posture were the positioning of his right arm, which stretched upward, and the absence of information about his left arm and hand. The position of the left arm is the key to this spirit journey, and undoubtedly information about this position was purposely withheld by the Egyptian priests who, by that time, were retaining the secrets of spirit journeying for themselves.

The group of us at the Cuyamungue Institute had some difficulty with our early experiences of this posture because the position of our left thumbs was wrong. Once this was corrected, getting out of our bodies was accomplished much more easily. One person described this process as beginning with a tingling in the head; then something reaches down from the head into the midsection and pulls, so that conscious awareness is pulled right out of the body through the top of the head. Leaving the body can also occur through the genitals, the solar plexus, the heart, or the middle of the forehead.

Using this pose, the sensation of leaving the body is experienced in many ways. Following are various experiences culled from the comments of workshop participants: "I felt like I was a rocket, moving very, very fast." "I shed my outer covering and became a white bird." "I saw a cross-bow, but when the arrow was shot it became a bird." "There was a lion that was sprouting wings as it was running up the dark stairs of my spine, and once it reached the top there was an opening into the bright sunshine." "I became a white bird with rainbow wings."

Once out of the body and soaring into the Sky World, many experiences become possible. Often people's stories of these journeys have an extraordinary beauty, although it is not necessarily visual. Many include sounds as well as visceral and kinesthetic sensations, with varying emphasis, just as in ordinary reality. Following is one of my experiences in this posture:

> I saw a huge snowy-topped mountain encircled with stars like the Paramount Pictures logo—except we were the stars and were dancing in a circle around the peak; we joined hands and flew out into the stars to bring back gifts for our friends.

The most common experience is to be a bird or fly with a bird. The bird mask and staff of the Lascaux shaman predicted this. Freedom of flight and powerful flows of energy are characteristic of the Lascaux Cave posture. Pamela described seeing all of her animal spirit allies coming through the sky:

> They were all pure white. I had body sensations—physical butterfly feelings—sexual. Then I could see myself lying, and I could see energy move

through and around me, up through my eyes, and [then] it was a light show. The sexual feelings were not overwhelming, just there. It seemed to last forever.

Excitedly, Pamela drew a picture of herself in the newly created energy field. It resembled the images depicting the inner workings of an atom.

There is much to learn about the uses of this posture. It produces a great deal of energy and seems to connect with forces both within the body and in the universe. The sexual sensations Pamela felt are common, suggesting arousal of the lower chakras where the life force is said to enter and be distributed throughout the body. Pamela's allies let her know that they were available to help, and their appearance as "pure white" confirmed that they were totally in spirit form.

DESCRIPTION

To accomplish this posture, your body must be positioned at exactly a 37-degree angle. While it is possible to rig up support with a chair and pillows, you may consider constructing a stand from plywood to allow you to rest at the proper angle. At the Cuyamungue Institute, these platforms are affectionately dubbed "launching pads."

Your feet should be parallel, slightly apart, and at a 90-degree angle to your legs. Lean your body against the support at a 37-degree angle. Stretch your left arm beside your body, with your elbow locked. Relax your fingers, but keep your left thumb stiff, so that a straight line can be drawn from your shoulder, through your elbow and wrist, and to the tip of your thumb. Rest your right arm beside your body and at a 37-degree angle from your body. Face the palm of your right hand toward your thigh, and rest your right thumb on top of your fingers. Keep your head facing forward but rest back on the support structure, with your eyes closed.

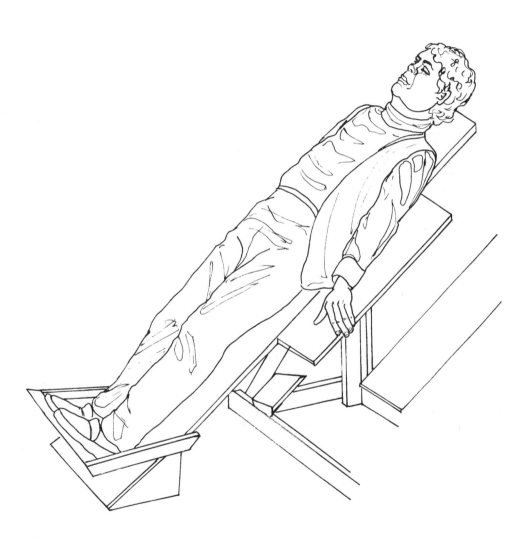

The Long Man of Wilmington Posture

On the north side of Windover Hill, on the east end of South Downs near the town of Wilmington in Sussex, England, there is a huge petroglyph. It is of a man seventy meters tall who holds a stake on either side of his body. It has been estimated that this drawing is between 2000 and 2500 years old. What is he doing there?

Dr. Goodman proposes that as horticultural peoples lost their powerful ability to make spirit journeys to bring their world back into balance, they began to take actions in ordinary reality, hoping that there would be a beneficial result in Alternate Reality. [37] Imbalances in the ordinary world were believed to create torn places in the web of energy that supported all of material existence, "a very complex multidimensional matrix." She suggests that for a while these people tried to represent the patterns of this matrix in abstract geometric forms on the face of the Earth, in hopes that those forms would impose themselves on Alternate Reality. Around the world, gigantism, that is, the creation of huge forms and heads at ritual sites, appeared for a discrete time in history, then disappeared. The Long Man of Wilmington took his place on the cliff of Windover Hill about this time.

The first experience with this posture at the Cuyamungue Institute took place in the kiva with a group of ten people who had been journeying in Alternate Reality for a number of years. Perhaps we were influenced by knowing that the Long Man of Wilmington was inscribed in a cliff by the sea. Almost everyone saw cliffs or whitecaps or seagulls, or was standing on a cliff overlooking the sea with seabirds crying. Everyone also commented on hearing tones—so many tones, said Norma, "that the kiva was alive with sounds." One person heard a high-pitched drum and bell; another heard a high-pitched humming with which her heart and the sound of the drumming resonated; a third described the sound as flute-like. Judy understood that if she were to fine-tune the poles (the six-foot dowels we grasped in our hands) with the humming, it was possible to have access to "a door to wherever I want to go."

We all agreed that an energy seemed to rise from the poles. Jan said we had become sending and receiving stations, and that by adjusting our poles and our bodies we could connect and align with something at another level of reality. The poles gave us balance, so that we could become portals or doorways; this would give some of us the ability to fly into space or to the edge of the cosmos. This expressed so well the reality of a spirit journey, in which we could learn to leave this reality and travel through doorways into other places in the multidimensional universe.

The journey took Robinette briefly back in time to a cold place where a group of people in heavy skins were doing a ceremony. They were worried about the changes in their lives, as their culture was transitioning. To her, the huge drawing on the cliff was a sign that said of these people, "we have this knowledge; we live under the protection of this knowledge." I, too, saw a ceremony on a cold, gray beach. It was a ceremony I seemed to recognize from the long distant past, and as it concluded the people gathered around the fire turned to me and said, "We have waited so long for you to return." Returning to the kiva after the trance, I listened as Cara spoke of waiting a very long time, the mythical time "from sunrise to sunset," for something or someone. It seemed as though we had gone back to the time when the Long Man of Wilmington was created to strengthen the people's ability to tune into the higher frequencies of other dimensions—to be aligned with the beings of Alternate Reality.

We were all hot during the trance, and most of us described bright light and energy. Bolts of lightning or blue-white light shot through Norma and into the ground as she aligned her body with the higher levels. Gwyn was propelled to the edges of the cosmos and felt bolts of lightning sending white-hot energy; then all the bolts became thunderbeings who chanted, "You have come among us. You have come among us." We had, indeed, learned to journey to their realms.

DESCRIPTION

This posture requires props: two thin sticks or dowels, each about six feet long. Position these staves at each side of your body, and grasp each stave with your hand at a place just above shoulder level. Your left hand should be slightly higher than your right hand. In a normal standing position, with your knees relaxed, extend your right foot forward and angle it slightly to the right.

This tends to put a little more weight on your left leg. Look straight ahead with your eyes closed. This positioning creates a 37-degree angle in your right arm, with your elbow as the axis. This 37-degree angle is the hallmark of spirit journeys.

THE PRIESTESS OF MALTA POSTURE

Around 5000 years ago, the people who lived on the island of Malta carved into the rock an underground temple that is today called the Hypogeum. Within the temple have been found figurines in the Priestess of Malta posture, surrounded by piles of skeletons. Dr. Goodman speculates that the shamanesses of Malta followed the tradition of the Buryat of Central Asia. When a person dies, the Buryat shaman guides the person's soul on a journey over the world in which she or he lived and is now preparing to leave. In this way the person's soul can be reminded of the beauty of its homeland in this life. Then the soul is taken to the entrance to the Realm of the Dead, to leave this world and move on to a new home.

The Priestess of Malta posture takes a practitioner on a spirit journey, neither up to the Sky World nor down to the Lower World, but across the Middle World, which is the spirit counterpart of the daily environment. In one trance, I was taken to the American Southwest, to the Arctic regions, to Polynesia, China, and the savannahs of East Africa. When I asked, "Why do we do this?" the reply was, "To survey the Earth to see how she's doing."

The experience of flying is common with the Priestess of Malta posture. One woman described a rocking sensation that seemed to her like something that would be felt by a bird. When she let go, she said the sensation of soaring was a wonderful feeling. On her journey, she visited a city with tall buildings that she identified as Machu Picchu. At the same workshop, Ildiko spoke of the sensation of growing wide, yellow wings. She felt herself going through a tunnel, very fast, then found herself in Transylvania, where she was born. Judy was in a mirrored room in Persia. There was no experience of flying in her trance. She had more of an inner experience, "as if I were in the center of a diamond."

People also have occasional sensations of being dead, or more accurately of being buried. In one trance, I was lying inside a small stone building with a dirt floor. I thought at first it was a cell, but it seemed more benign than a prison. Later a group of women stood over me, handling my body. Then I was laid on a cart and carried over stone streets. In the next scene, I was laid next to the stones of a small fire. After the fire died, I cooled down and was picked up and carried away.

The unique qualities of the rituals associated with the priestesses of Malta come to life in this trance experience shared by Pamela:

> I saw a temple or one side of it, a corner. It glowed against the late-evening, dark hills and blue, pink, purple sky and river. It was on a hill.

There were women in white, flowing, long, sleeveless dresses and some sort of headdress. I really saw only one but knew there were others. Then a huge eaglelike bird seemed to come close and have something in its feet . . . like a ritual offering of some sort. Then I saw a group of lion cubs all curled up.

Then I was back at the temple and there was a beautiful lionness with the priestesses. . . . I saw a huge snake . . . and a white slab with scrolls on it. . . . I realized I was watching a ritual/ceremony and asked what it was about. I received "cleansing transformation" as my answer. At one point she [the priestess] seemed to turn everything bright as if making daylight. Then she danced and the eagle soared, the lionness walked, and the snake seemed to stay upright. How perfect! At the end she raised her hands to God and the tape ended!

With the conclusion of the rattling tape, Pamela emerged from the trance on cue.

DESCRIPTION

This is a standing posture. Place your feet parallel, slightly apart, with your toes pointing straight ahead. Hold your right arm stiffly beside your body with your elbow locked. Hold your left upper arm close to your body. Bending your left elbow to a 90-degree angle, bring your left palm against your waist. Face forward with your eyes closed.

THE SAMI LOWER WORLD POSTURE

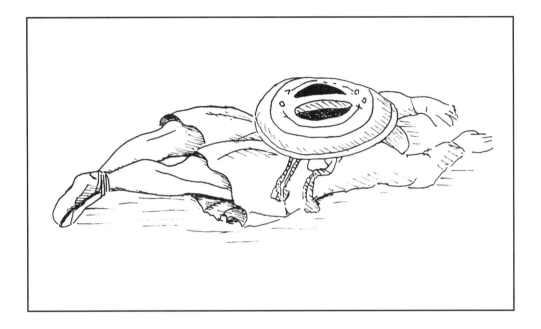

A drawing of this posture serves as an illustration for a German traveler's journal published in 1673. The shaman lying in the posture belongs to the tribe of nomadic reindeer herders of northern Europe, known as the Sami, who live in what is known as Lapland. These people are apparently close enough to their hunter ancestors to retain their shamanistic methods for undertaking a spirit journey. In the book's illustration, the shaman lies face down with his drum tied to his back. His arms extend forward, as though he is diving, and his crossed feet are tied together. An assistant is seated beside him, using a T-shaped bone to thump against a round, flat, hide-covered drum decorated with glyphs. These glyphs or symbols are images that condense information and memories—instructions about

where the shaman travels on his journeys, how to get there, and how to return. Each image might be thought of as a doorway through which the shaman passes as he begins his journey.

As you make your own spirit journey with the Sami posture, you too have to find the doorway through which you can pass. There are many images for showing you the way down—tunnels and whirlwinds and downward spirals. All are images through which you can do what Gwyn once described as "sliding down the World Tree into the Lower World." You must find a way for going down into the Earth and the Lower World below, remembering of course that your notions of "above" and "below" are human constructs. These concepts allow you to keep your bearings, your sense of order and direction in a larger universe in which space and time do not exist in the ways you tend to think of them.

Consistently, the entrance to the Lower World seems dark to those who make the journey, at least using this posture. For Pam, the entrance was a black whirlpool. As she moved down, caught in the whirlpool, a masked Indian dancer beckoned and then guided her through the trance, eventually leading her up and out of the Lower World, back into the Middle World where she lives. Once I looked in vain for a tunnel or cave entrance, then realized I could just lie down on the ground. I sank into the white snow and then into the darkness of the Earth, gradually sinking until I was among the roots of the plants and trees and all things.

Another time, a tunnel took me into cold, dark water, where I sank to the bottom of the ocean and became an ancient life form. Backward I went through evolution, until I was only a molecule. Finally, in a subatomic state, I heard these lines:

> Before time began,
> Out of me the years roll,
> Out of me God and man,
> I am ancient and whole.

I recognized these words as being from a poem entitled "Hertha," by the Victorian poet Swinburne. Hertha was an ancient Germanic goddess of the Earth, a bearer of fertility and growth. Swinburne saw her as even more than this—as the feminine matrix that brought atoms and molecules together to form the material world so familiar to us. So for me, the journey to the Lower World went back to the beginning of matter, in the molecular sense, and connected me with a time before God and man as known by the Victorian city dwellers.

At the Cuyamungue Institute, we often use this posture at the beginning of a Masked Trance Dance to journey to the Lower World to meet one of the animal spirits who live there. Usually, many animals will appear, but one animal will predominate and offer a special experience. However, if we have an intention of meeting a particular animal, we may look too hard. One woman saw a buffalo mask, the head of a bird, a bear's head, a coyote, and a dolphin:

> None of these seemed to be inviting me, however. I began to wonder [if I would find out which animal I should make a mask of], reminding myself I could do another trip, using the South American posture. I felt more of a sense of gliding, drifting, as earlier. As I stayed with the sensation, I realized I was a whale. I was the whale. So I did not see the whale, but rather felt its sensations throughout the trance, not recognizing until the end that the whale had already invited me, embraced me in a sense, allowing me to become part of its slow, vast being. I was expecting to see something and nearly overlooked my nonvisual experience.

In a trance that was not part of a Masked Trance Dance, both Carol and Pamela saw masked dancers as they made a spirit journey with the Sami Lower World posture. As Carol reported:

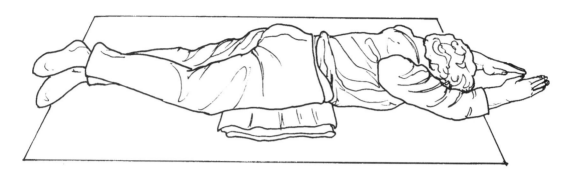

> I was aware of whiteness all over and then a pup tent rose up out of
> the snow and I thought I should go into the dark entrance. I followed peo-
> ple with animal skins on their backs—I couldn't see any faces. I was very
> aware of a snow leopard. Then the figures were dancing—much differently
> from any I've ever seen. They danced very vigorously with knees deeply
> bent. They wore wooden masks of different animals.

It is common for people using this posture to see the contrast of
white and dark. The white may be snow, light, icebergs, a polar bear, a
herd of white horses, or white buffalo. Often people see the dark entrance
to the Lower World standing out against whiteness. In a group, however,
some people may see whiteness while others see the darkness.

In one group of newcomers, the journey to the Sami Lower World
brought a variety of experiences. Jeff was in a familiar jungle with a jaguar, whom he already knew from earlier dreams and imagery, leading him
as a guide and companion. David described a maternal presence and a
waterfall. Marcia focused on feeling joyful and said, "it was as though I
had been let out for recess." Another woman saw her son's dog that had
died. Elizabeth wandered into a cave where a group of aboriginal men
were circled around a fire in a ritual. This wide array of images, all of

which were experienced in the Lower World, suggests that it is best not to have too rigid an expectation of what might be encountered in such journeys.

The assistant of the Lapp shaman in the German drawing had a drum covered with glyphs and symbols. At a recent Masked Trance Dance in Ohio, several people mentioned seeing in trance stone carvings and stick drawings. In the same trance, Judith met an old woman in a ceremonial hogan who wanted to tell her "the ancient stories of the bones." Since these workshop participants had not seen the old German illustration, their visions imply that there is more to learn about the role of the assistant, his bone drumming stick, and the symbols on his drum. At the Cuyamungue Institute, we have no other examples of this posture and therefore no other ethnographic information to enrich our understanding. We must rely on our continuing experiences in the Sami posture to give us answers.

DESCRIPTION

Lie down on the floor or on a mat, face down, with both arms extended forward, your right arm extended just a little bit farther than your left. Gently cup your hands and place them palms down, about five inches apart. Point your fingers slightly toward each other, as though they are "pigeon-toed." Extend your legs, with your right foot placed on top of your left foot, so your feet are crossed at the ankles. You may place a small pillow under your pelvis to make yourself more comfortable in this position. Turn your head to the right.

The original drawing of this posture shows the shaman's flat round drum resting on his back and covering most of his head. You can simulate the drum with a pillow or a wreath woven from pliable branches, but this is not necessary to accomplish the trance.

THE SOUTH AMERICAN LOWER WORLD POSTURE

In his book *The Way of the Shaman*,[38] Michael Harner tells of being taught shamanic practices by the Jivaro Indians in Ecuador. This posture, which involves lying on the back with the left arm covering the eyes, is one he teaches in his workshops on shamanic journeying and counseling. While he often instructs his students to visualize a cave or other underground opening, at the Cuyamungue Institute we have found this suggestion unnecessary. Most people find their way to the Lower World using this posture whether they visualize the entrance at the outset or not. From the reports of workshop participants, we know the Lower World can be entered through a cave, a flower, a vulva, a hollow tree, stairs, a tunnel, a chute, a water slide, or a spiral of light, or by sinking into the Earth. With every workshop, a new method is introduced. There may be turbulence at the entrance—a swirling energy or fog or water—which must be entered and passed through in order to undertake the journey to the Lower World.

People who live in cities and towns have a tendency to fear the Lower World. The traditions from the agricultural religions of recent ancestors teach that Hell is in the Lower World and that animal spirits are associated with demons or satanic practices. In addition, the secular world has its own variety of fears, especially the fear of losing control of the mind by journeying too far from the familiar world of ego dominance. This fear of becoming insane was projected by Julie as she confessed, "[There was] anxiety of not wanting to let go—a pounding in my head as I tried to control what was happening." She was afraid of losing control of herself—of plummeting into a dark unknown where her ego could not survive. Courage, as well as a great trust in her Higher Power and in the rest of the group, supported her as she faced this fear—until she was able to release herself to the trance. In a later experience, she reported a beautiful journey of changing form until she became at last the essence of a rose, with no form or ego.

Others who have been initially fearful have called on the help of animal friends, finding protection, for instance, in the wings of Eagle, or the comforting sound of the rattle. In the United States, we are so reliant on being independent and in control that many, many people raised in our culture cannot imagine retaining their identities otherwise. I suspect that it is deeply empowering to discover that we keep our individuality and integrity when we journey beyond the familiar world, even though the remaining sense of self is often not what we imagined it would be.

In my own early experience with this posture, I arrived in a desert and was walking across three logs that stretched across a small gully. I was about halfway across when the logs became a narrow and unsteady bridge over a deep chasm in a mountainous jungle. Quaking with a fear of great heights, I crossed to the other side, only to face a skull and crossbones, a further warning and threat of danger. Unusually determined, I asked permission to pass through the entrance, which was clouded with fog. Then I found myself nose to nose with a little seal, and my fears dissolved as I was invited to join in the play of young sea animals. The imagery revealed that I had begun my journey to the Lower World freely and with great acceptance. Then, when I was halfway across the bridge, too far to easily turn back, the doubts and fears began. Had I somehow gone too far this time? Was my friend right who told me she prayed for my soul (because I was going into trance)? Would I be banished from the metaphysical teachings that had been my spiritual mainstay for a decade? Facing the fog of questions, I decided I wanted to go on. The other reality then became not foreboding to me at all but as natural and inviting as a baby seal and playful otters.

There are others who enter the Lower World easily. This was Mary's first trance experience with a ritual posture:

> The sound of the rattle brought an image of an Indian kachina dancer with blue feathers on his face. He was dancing around a fire. Then I became a lot of different animals: an eagle, a bear, a snake. I shifted back and forth from the dancer to the animals. I was filled with the feeling of being at one with nature. I could see through the eyes of the animals and feel how they felt.

Using this posture is the simplest way to make the journey to the

Lower World. In this posture, contrary to the usual experience of becoming very hot in trance, people often report feeling cool as they make their descent: "There was a cool wind blowing over me, and it was comforting." "I am in a cool wooded place." "Earlier my eyes were burning. Then I began to get cool, and I felt like I was dying, calm and pleasant." Because the Realm of the Dead is in the Lower World, people sometimes meet family or friends who have died, but this is not a grim experience. Once, in this posture, I saw a funeral procession and then became the body on the bier. I was buried in the ground, then "climbed up the sod to a beautiful scene of mountains and a valley full of orange and black butterflies." It was a wonderful experience, and I have returned to that valley in many trances since.

At the Cuyamungue Institute, we use this posture, as well as the Sami Lower World posture, at the beginning of the Masked Trance Dance to invite an animal spirit to befriend us. We then make a mask and costume of this animal. We live in close harmony with the animal during the week, and finally share in its reality during the metamorphosis phase of the dance itself. It is common for people to see a lot of animals in this posture's trance before finding the one that will be the teacher and companion for the week. Even when the posture is not done as part of a dance workshop, dancing is sometimes incorporated into the trance. Carol reported:

> I saw a winding river and then a whirlpool that took me to the Lower World. I saw dogs standing guard. Then I was Badger, Wolf, Cougar, and then people dancing with animal masks. . . . Then I was a shaft of light and/or water that led me out of the Lower World.

In the traditions of shamans from Siberia, Australia, and South America, illness is believed to occur when the soul is separated from the body. Healing is accomplished by descending to the Lower World to

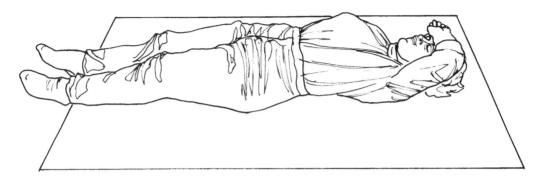

retrieve the lost soul. Soul retrieval is not taught at the Cuyamungue Institute. However, in this particular spirit journey, it is not unusual for people to experience various kinds of healing. Wyn said, "My ears were resonating with the drum, as though my tubes were being unclogged." Another woman said she felt vibrations throughout her body. Her knee, which had been injured in an accident, hurt; however, after the trance, she felt better. Another woman, with arthritis, spoke of a warm pleasant tingling in her knees, while another felt continual twitching in an injured toe, as though it were receiving a treatment. The healing can also be emotional. In one workshop, a participant said, "A snake ate up my irritability." Other people receive special messages that are healing, like "Don't try to get nourishment from streams that are already dry." One message I especially liked was from a woman who said, "[I was told by the spirits] the outer life is just a workshop, don't take it too seriously. Then I was being rattled over and healed."

DESCRIPTION

Lie down on the floor or on a mat with your back against the floor. Do not elevate your head with a pillow. If you have a spinal problem, you can alleviate discomfort by putting a small pillow under your knees. Allow your right arm to lie beside your body in a natural, relaxed position. Raise your left arm and allow the back of your left hand to rest on the middle of your fore-head. Remove any jewelry, such as rings or bracelets, that might cause a distraction.

Michael Harner describes your left arm and hand as being positioned so that, if a light were shining from beyond the top of your head, your hand would shield your eyes from the light. Be sure that your forearm puts no pressure on your eyes, however. As always, your eyes should be closed.

THE REALM OF THE DEAD POSTURE

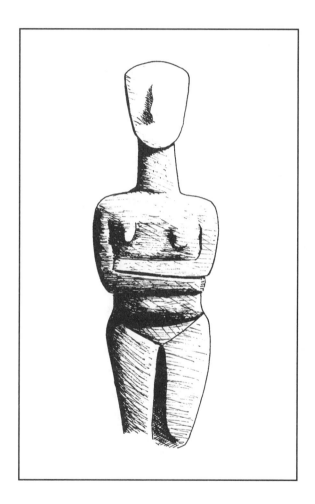

A wonderful example of a figure in this posture was found in the Baden-Wuerttemberg region in Germany. Dating from the fifth century B.C., it is the figure of a young warrior, standing about five feet tall, carved in sandstone. He was on a hill that was a common grave, and the hill was encircled with stone slabs.

Our experiences with this posture at the Cuyamungue Institute have shown us that it can mediate experiences of dying and journeys into the Realm of the Dead. We have speculated that the shamans from the Hallstatt tradition used this posture to prepare warriors for battle. The warriors might have been instructed about the Realm of the Dead during the trance so that they would not fear dying. Having already made the journey into the Realm of the Dead, they would not have experienced it as a fearful and unknown place. They would have known what to expect from dying and what part of themselves continued after death, and they would have experienced taking on a new form in the other reality. With nothing to fear from death, they could have fought courageously.

Three thousand years earlier, on the Cyclades, north of Crete, little figurines of this posture were traditionally placed in the graves of both men and women. Almost all of these statues that have been found are female, and they vary slightly from the Hallstatt warrior in that the left arm is lowered to a position just parallel to the right arm, which lies along the waistline. Because the facial features and physical characteristics of the figurines vary, Dr. Goodman suggests that they probably represent specific local shamanesses whose job it was to take the spirits of those who had died to the Realm of the Dead. She comments, "It was clearly a woman's office; men took it over only under exceptional circumstances."[39] The role of guiding the spirits of the dead is more clearly played out in the Psychopomp posture. In this ritual posture, workshop participants are more likely to report making the journey themselves.

Following is one workshop participant's trance experience using the Realm of the Dead posture:

> My eyes are closed and I am walking along a path, with light to the
> left and darkness to the right—it is the road between the two worlds. The
> rattle urges me on. Gradually I find myself turning right, into a land of gray

and fog. . . . Eventually I tumble down a steep bank of shale and pebbles. Like a rag doll I fall. At the bottom there is nothing; I am alone. I sift through bones and ashes and find a skull that I put on, but then I sneeze and give myself away as a visitor, instead of someone who had really died. There are others behind me marching through this land. We come to a fire and enter willingly. The smoke is my spirit, rising above this realm and eventually above all the Earth, first into a place of pink and blue clouds. I am going home! Slowly, gradually, I feel myself rising into a reunion. The sadness of saying goodbye is replaced by tears of joy. . . . The slowness of the passage is all worth it now, none of it matters anymore. All the aloneness and not knowing no longer matter.

In a typical trance, the traveler wanders in desolate areas, finally coming to a deep pit in which various spirits are encountered. Often the person describes having skin and muscle torn off until she or he is only bones. But eventually something changes and the journeyer begins to rise into a new form and a new life. Because it is easier to get down to the Realm of the Dead than it is to return, it is wise to ask a spirit helper, an animal spirit friend, to go along on the journey. Bear is always a good helper in situations such as these. In one person's experience, Bear ate the one who had died and then regurgitated the soul as another form into another unknown realm. The shamaness figurines were most likely helpers for the people of the Cyclades, giving support for their transformation into new life after death.

One variation on this posture appears in a catalogue from a Mexican art exhibit in Venice, Italy. It is a seated figure, and a garment covers the legs, making it impossible to tell which leg is crossed in front of the other. This variation facilitates a similar kind of trance to that described above. One woman shared what happened to her:

At the beginning, I felt a brief rocking, but then nothing. I kept feeling a desire to collapse physically. Finally I could collapse in my subtle bod-

ies and still keep the posture. When I did, I said to myself, "This is like dying and rotting and turning into ashes." Then I took on the form of the statue, with its beady eyes and sneering demeanor, and related to a different worldview. Death is a stage, when decay is the developmental task. It

seemed dangerous to go too far into this, and I called for help. Bear came and I was brought back. My cat came to the edge of the other side and hissed at me.

DESCRIPTION

This is a standing posture. Stand with your feet parallel, about six inches apart, and point your toes straight ahead. Keep your knees slightly bent. Put your right hand over your waist, with the ball of your hand covering your navel and your middle finger extending along your waistline. Place your left arm against your chest, with the palm of your hand against your chest, so that it is just above your right arm and parallel to it. Your upper arms should be relaxed and close to your body. Face forward, with your eyes closed.

Variant: *Some figures in this posture indicate that you should place your left hand palm down against your chest so that the ball of your hand is at the midpoint between your breasts and your fingers are pointing toward your right shoulder.*

Another variation, a sitting version, was mentioned above. Keep your arms parallel, with your left arm resting on top of your right, and your left hand not quite covering your left breast. Cross your legs; it is not clear which is in front. At the Cuyamungue Institute, we have crossed the left leg in front of the right leg.

THE VENUS OF GALGENBERG POSTURE

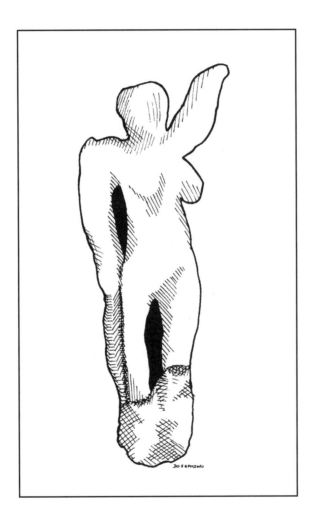

The remarkable little figure from which this posture is taken is sculpted from slate. She was discovered in 1988 at an archaeological site near the town of Krems on the Danube River. Standing only 2¾ inches

tall, she is nearly 32,000 years old, making her pose the oldest ritual posture yet to be identified. She is named the Venus of Galgenberg, after the site where she was found. When Dr. Goodman first received a photograph of the figure, she recognized that the figure's upstretched left arm formed a 37-degree angle with her head and torso, linking her with the bird-mask shaman found in the Lascaux Cave. She knew that the Lascaux Cave posture mediated a spirit-journey trance to the Sky World. Would the Venus of Galgenberg do the same?

The first experience with this posture took place at a workshop in Columbus, Ohio. Dr. Goodman documented the reports of the twenty-three workshop participants in *Jewels on the Path*.[40] What we discovered is that this Venus is the great-grandmother of postures, taking people to the Tree of the World as does the Calling the Spirits posture. It sends people on journeys to the Lower World, the Realm of the Dead, and to the Sky World, offering them the possibility of becoming active helpers in sustaining the balance of the universe. With all of this going on, it is not surprising that almost everyone has a strong reaction to using this posture. People report feeling hot in the trances induced by most postures, especially when healing is taking place. When using the Venus of Galgenberg posture, however, people report being extremely hot, to the point that they are dripping with perspiration. It is also a painful posture, partly because of the difficulty of keeping the left arm raised for fifteen minutes. The pain is also related to the intense energy flowing through the body during the trance.

Once, against my friend MaryAnna's advice, I undertook this trance alone and was unable to maintain the posture for the full duration of the rattling tape because I was in so much pain. A second time, Judy accompanied me, and it was a difficult but tolerable journey for each of us. A few weeks later, at a Masked Trance Dance, when we used the Venus of Galgenberg posture again, Judy commented that it was much easier with nine of us than with two.

The 37-degree angle is formed at the point where the line of the arm and the line of the head and spine meet, which is at the heart. In my first experience with this posture, it felt like a bolt of lightning passed through my body. In my journal, I wrote, "A huge shot of energy came down my left arm and side, across my chest and heart; it came down the right side to be grounded by the stick I held in my right hand." At the same workshop, Jan reported:

> During breathing I had a great deal of energy in my sternum, my heart center. And when the rattle started I first became very relaxed in the posture. As soon as I became relaxed, my heart center, where I felt that energy, split open. And when it split open, it was like a combustion fire that just started at that point.[41]

Later, Jan had a physical reaction to the trance: red sensitive blotches appeared around her breasts, on top of her feet, and inside her legs. It took several days of cool compresses and rest to alleviate the condition. While a reaction such as this is not common, it is worth noting. Individuals with sensitive physical systems and strong response to the altered conditions of trance may experience physiological responses to postures that mediate powerful journeys into Alternate Reality. Healers familiar with herbs and techniques for balancing energy should be consulted under conditions such as these.

Many people report energy flowing both up and down their bodies. They feel themselves open up, and often experience genital stimulation. Once, in trance, I saw myself standing beside a huge erect penis that eventually ejaculated me into the void—into the stars and the darkness. It is said that the second chakra, the sexual center, transmits the life force through the physical and auric bodies. Sexual stimulation during trance may be an indication that the flow of the life force is expanding to sustain the spirit journey and the multiple tasks that are inherent to this posture.

The most significant discovery that came from the early experience with the Venus of Galgenberg posture in Columbus was that we, as humans, help keep the Earth in alignment with "the patterns in the stars." Jan said:

> [I was taken to] a very complex multidimensional matrix . . . an extremely complicated pattern. I was travelling along the lines and then between the spaces. . . . Then there was a point at which I exploded into a seed of light. . . . I wanted to make a sound at another level to help direct and move myself as light. It wasn't a continuous sound, but a sound that would come up and increase and decrease every once in a while. And when I did that, that seemed to help make shifts or turns or connections between parts of the matrix that hadn't been connected before.

Similarly, during the same trance, I found myself in the Council of Trees:

> I tried to stay focused. The council meeting was at such a deep level—down to the depths and into the stars—and I realized that the trees were trying to align to a pattern in the stars, and that I could do that, too, in my own body—body, trees, Earth, stars, all in alignment, and then energy could flood through. "Is that all there is?" I asked. A somewhat surprised and stern voice said, "What do you mean? This is all there is—this aligning in greater patterns for the energy to move through—that is the meaning in it all."

Later experiences with this posture were not as specifically focused on learning *what* to do as they were on actual doing. Judy saw a narrow band of energy coming from the sun, down through her body, and through the stick in her hand into the ground. She was urged to wrap her raised arm around a column of golden light, and tears came welling up at the wonderfulness of it. The rattle seemed to pick up speed, and her arm was trying to reach further into the sky "when a huge ring of energy came down around us, up through the center as a volcano, and shot up to the sky."

During one trance, in an archetypal drama of the hungry, abused children of the Earth, Judith saw those of us using the Venus of Galgenberg posture lighting a fire and finding places to lie down to sleep:

> We each held a baby against our breasts. All of our dreams became the smoke and covered the Earth like a quilt. Included were the memories of all who ever lived here and all the animals gathered around the fire, watching.

In other words, we can journey to the Sky World to find the patterns that are the original intention for the Earth. We can draw the energy of those patterns down to the Earth, helping to bring ourselves, the Earth, and all the other children of the Earth into better alignment with these patterns. This was a task once held by medicine people, but their presence has diminished since the old days. Now it is possible for all of us to learn, in whatever small ways we are capable, how to help bring back the balance. It is sometimes painful, physically and emotionally. It is a difficult task, especially for us who are untrained, but we have help.

Sometimes we can help each other. When one group of us used the Venus of Galgenberg posture to help a friend prepare for his vision quest, I felt Judy's presence beside me, and "her breathing gave me strength." Helpers can also come from the other realms. One frequent helper is the eagle, who in many traditions is the one who connects the Earth with the sky worlds. One woman, with tears in her eyes, said, "I saw briefly but clearly the eagle kachina. Not a mask but the real thing, with soft, small feathers. It helped me know the level of clarity and purity with which we are trying to connect."

DESCRIPTION

This is a standing posture. Stand with your left leg straight, and your left foot facing forward. Bend your right leg at the knee, with your right foot angled slightly away from your body. With your right hand, hold a stick and point it so that it extends to just above the ground. Grasp the stick with your forefinger extended along its length. Raise your left arm, cup your hand, and face the palm of the hand toward your body; your arm forms a 37-degree angle with a vertical line extending through your head and spine. Raise your head and turn it toward the left. Allow your eyes to gaze toward your raised hand even though they remain closed.

Initiation:
Death and Rebirth

The term *initiation* implies ritual or ceremony that marks a passing—from one phase of life to the next, or from a stage of innocence to one of knowing. Our urban culture seems to contain only the faded remnants of initiation rituals, leaving us longing for the richly saturated colors of the real things. Still, we have ceremonies for marking the seasons of our lives. High school graduates, with their fresh young faces, march down aisles to receive diplomas. We are acknowledging these young people as entering an adult phase of their lives. They have completed a difficult undertaking, their years of education, and are being welcomed into the adult world of jobs and college, marriage and families. We know that many high school graduates are not ready for the responsibilities of adulthood and that their initiation task, of completing high school, has not necessarily prepared them for what lies ahead. Some are already working; others already have children. As a true initiation, their graduation may not mean much. Nevertheless, something is different, and the graduation ceremony and the parties that surround it are our culture's way of declaring that a passage has been made.

An initiation marks a transition into a new way of being in the world. The celebration of menarche proclaims a natural initiation, brought on by the changes in a young girl's body that make her a woman. A rite of passage for an adolescent boy is designed to mimic the natural transition—marking his body in circumcision for instance, and forcing him to make a break from the emotional bond with his mother.

When they are involved with entrance into adult life, initiations are focused primarily on the acquisition of new knowledge and the understanding of our place in the grand scheme of things. The spiritual quest of almost every culture is the revelation of the mysteries of life. Most of us are only kindergartners when it comes to sacred wisdom. Many of us in the United States and around the world have begun to borrow from the traditions of Native Americans: the vision quest, the process of shield-making, and various other methods for learning who we are and finding our paths. In the capable hands of those who have been trained in these traditions, these are helpful tools, gratefully received. For many others of us, psychotherapy has become our culture's rite of passage. Through the therapeutic process, we learn about who we really are and find meanings with which to lay solid foundations for our lives.

What was the wisdom our ancestors possessed that was passed along from grandmother to younger daughter, from wise one to student, from master to initiate? Some might argue that it is impossible to know this wisdom, that the answers to the mysteries have long been lost and we can only hope for the discovery of ancient manuscripts if we would know the ancient truths, that the old wise ones are dying and taking their secrets with them. Yet out of the dark pool of hidden wisdom rises the experience of ecstatic trance, used for millennia as a source of both knowledge and experience. The beauty of the ritual body postures is that ecstatic trance teaches the sacred truths in a language understandable by city dwellers or agriculturalists. And so the ageless questions can be asked again, and answers can be given that make sense to our urban minds, that are relevant to us.

We can begin with questions framed by Socrates: Where do I come from? Where am I going? Within the context of the initiation postures, we can ask the first question using the Birthing posture. Its trance may take us to the Realm of the Unborn Spirits, the place where we all begin the journey of incarnation on the Earth plane, when we come into this life, as Wordsworth put it, "trailing clouds of glory from God which is our home." What each of us sees there will vary; what is important is that each of us can feel the freedom and anticipation of the soul waiting for a body to be made available, a family to welcome it. The Birthing posture may also offer the experience of being born, of being received into the community of family and ancestors, and of being suckled and nurtured.

Birth is the first initiation in this life; the final one is death. The spirit journey to the Realm of the Dead gives us a glimpse of where we are going. The initiation posture called the Psychopomp allows us to be of service to those who have recently died, escorting souls who have lost their way in the nether world, and helping them make the transition to their new home. Not only can we serve others by using this posture, but in the process we can learn a little more about what our own passing will be like when we ourselves die.

All of the initiation trances tell us something about the mystery of life and death and rebirth. The Feathered Serpent is a great and powerful feminine being. I often call upon her help in workshops to give the participants some group trance experiences that can be enacted in a psychodrama. An entire group can intentionally enter Alternate Reality together and return with a group story. Each person brings back a portion of the story, and together the group weaves the strands to create a drama or mythic story. The Feathered Serpent posture always produces a story about death and rebirth.

Last spring in Missoula, a group of twenty of us went on a trance journey past mountains and water and dark beings that looked out from the reeds. Finally we came upon the Feathered Serpent herself, who had gaping jaws that invited us to enter. With seven women forming the body of this formidable snake, we each stood before her, choosing to die to some part of ourselves. Then we entered her body. She swallowed us, and we died and emerged from her tail, undergoing a birth into a new life. All the while, the drumbeat and chanting maintained the universal heartbeat. As the workshop facilitator, it fell to me to be the midwife, and I marveled at every fresh, beautiful face that appeared before me as each person was reborn into my waiting arms.

When it was at last my turn to enter the mouth of the Feathered Serpent, I balked. I had not been thinking of what part of my own psyche I was willing to allow to die. A thought flashed through my mind: "I will die to my fear of economic insecurity." This is a line from one of the promises in the Alcoholics Anonymous Big Book. I felt the presence of many helping hands as I passed through the serpent's body and soaked up the nearly palpable energy that saturated the room. I felt good but didn't know what, if anything, had changed. Upon returning home, however, I found myself commenting to friends about how oddly comfortable I felt having a smaller client load, taking risks with projects that were valuable but likely to lose money, and accepting my husband losing his job. It was a significant change for me, and it has lasted. Skeptics may explain it differently, but I thank the Feathered Serpent and the ritual our little group created from the death-and-rebirth process that the serpent shared with us.

The Greek Youth and Maiden posture teaches us about death and rebirth from early Greek and Egyptian perspectives. The Lady of Thessaly posture offers a view of what the Earth was like in the early times and helps us understand the purpose for material existence. The Venus of Laussel posture gives an initiation into the Realm of the Dead and teaches about the creation of new forms.

THE BIRTHING POSTURE

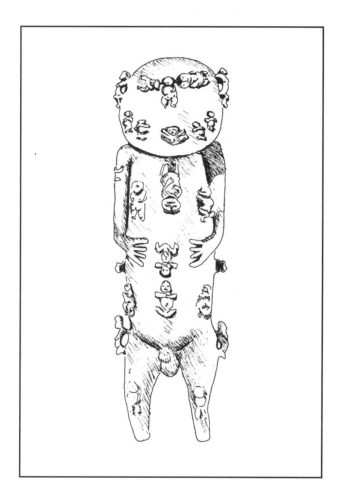

Figures in the Birthing posture have been found all over the world, from Negev, in the Near East, where they date from about 7000 years ago, to modern examples in central and western Africa, New Zealand, and throughout Polynesia. Figures atop a Bolivian jar provide one of the most wonderful images: a midwife sitting behind a mother in the process of giving birth. The midwife's hands are on the mother's abdomen, positioned in the same way as in the posture, while the infant's head is just beginning to emerge from the birth canal, into the hands of another midwife. Another immensely powerful figure of the Birthing posture is an eighteenth-century carving from Rurutu, one of the Austral Islands in Polynesia. Made from ironwood, the carving shows the god Tangaroa in the Birthing posture, apparently giving birth to other gods and humans who are shown as small figures carved into a variety of ritual postures all over his body. There are also two figures of kneeling versions of the posture, one on a Yoruba divination tray from Africa and the other from a catalogue of artworks from Mexico. Each figure is a woman with a distended belly and large breasts, indicating her condition of pregnancy.

The most significant rituals of hunter-gatherer and horticultural societies center around the celebration of birth.[42] These rituals focus on sex, the prerequisite for birth, and on invoking the ancestors of the tribe to welcome the infant who will perpetuate the People. However, in these rituals, the experience of the birth itself is often missing. The Birthing posture creates the opportunity to participate in various phases of the infant's birth process. These experiences may include: procreation, as the life enters the fetus so that it may develop into physical form; the arrival of the ancestors to witness and celebrate the birth; the unborn infant's dream of the world into which it is being born; the birth itself, often characterized by images of water, feelings of tiredness, a circle of light, or an opening; feelings of support as visitors arrive to greet the newly born child; and images of purple circles representing the breasts, signaling the presence of sustaining food and nurturance.

In one early workshop, a participant reported:

> Bright light with dark hole like a gullet or vacuum cleaner hose and small antlers over the top. Rejected idea of birth canal. Rattle was very loud. I wanted it to go away. Smaller rattle sound. I was drawn like an itch.

Pressure around the body. . . . A little fairylike person got on a swing and was trying to push to make it go faster.

A participant in a second workshop commented:

> I was down in a canyon, and there was a lot of purple. The purple became black and began to swirl. Then, as if looking at it from a bridge, I saw a blue bud coming up out of the canyon. I saw an eagle's eyes, then a light appeared in the pupil. I thought the slit looked like a vagina, but then rejected the idea. The slit had white figures in it. Suddenly I was cold, there was cold air swirling around me, and I saw more purple.

The white figures were those who had arrived to welcome the newborn, who felt the cold air outside the birth canal. Presumably, she also saw the purple nipple as she was drawn to the breast for food and the healing of her mother's loving touch.

In the initiation process of life, death, and rebirth, the Birthing posture actually comes both first and last in the sequence. We are born into this world, and after we live a life, we make the passage through the portals of death to spend time in the Realm of the Dead. We then rise again, taking a new form and a new life, which may mean being born again into this world and so beginning the cycle anew. Figures in the Birthing posture are in both male and female forms, emphasizing the universal experience of birthing, as well as the social and communal quality of the celebration of birth.

While people performing this posture usually experience some aspect of birthing from an infant's perspective, sometimes they feel what it is to be a mother. The following report is from a woman who had never conceived or delivered a child:

> I am very pregnant, with myself. Feel a great love for the baby in my belly, aware of her having come from the lovely realm of the unborn spirits.

She is afraid and I comfort her, and tell her I will protect her and help her be in this world. See her growing up, and my love for her is so great I nearly want to have a child.

Within six weeks, this woman was pregnant. Because of her experience, there has been conjecture about the usefulness of the Birthing posture in helping women conceive and carry pregnancies to full term, especially when they have had previous difficulties.

Recently, Judy and I questioned whether this posture could be used not only for the actual experience of pregnancy and delivery, but for the experience of birthing as a metaphor. Judy reported the following trance:

See pattern like walnut or brain with convolutions—a tunnel of energy—sexual energy in vagina. Spinning—underside of umbrella—under trees—spinning of potter's wheel. . . . Clay on potter's wheel—birthing a new idea or new being, may be a metaphor. Needing to center clay; hard work, and the piece will never be quite right if not centered. Can use it, but it won't be quite right—must start again.

Experiencing a tunnel and vaginal stimulation are common in this posture. The spinning Judy felt is similar to the experience of the infant beginning the birth process. The clay, however, was in Judy's hands; she was the one who was shaping the form, the container. Whatever she was to give birth to, the advice to her was to be centered, or it "won't be quite right," and she must "start again."

DESCRIPTION

Assume the standing position, with your feet parallel, about six inches apart, and your toes pointed forward. Be sure to keep your knees slightly bent. Place your hands palm down on either side of your abdomen, positioned so that the index finger of each hand is pointing toward your navel. The index

fingers should be about three to five inches apart, so your hands are holding your belly on either side. Keep your shoulders relaxed. Face forward with your eyes closed.

THE FEATHERED SERPENT POSTURE

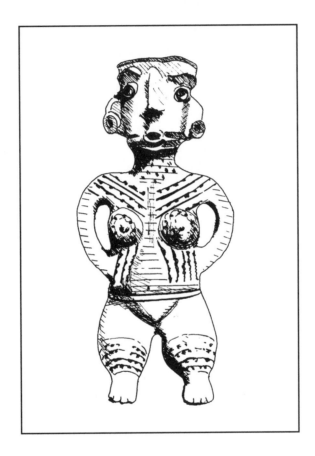

The Feathered Serpent is the mighty feminine source of life and fertility, the one who, in teaching the dance of life, takes us through the all-consuming cycles of death and rebirth. This posture can be traced to the hunter gatherers, among whom it is sometimes the task of the shaman to descend into a cave, which is the womb of the Earth, to create there on

the walls of the cave the likenesses of animals. In this way the soul essences of the animals can be lifted from the drawings and taken up to the world of the Sun, there to help Mother Earth propagate.

In central Yugoslavia, a 6000-year-old female figure was found in this posture, wearing a bird mask. On her chest was a glyph, a "V" bisected by a central line, elegantly describing the experience of falling into a hollow place and then rising to new life. The glyph also represented the vagina, from which life in this world emerges. Other examples of the Feathered Serpent posture have been found in Siberian petroglyphs dating from 5000 B.C., in clay figures of pre-Columbian grave sites in eastern Peru, and in copper cutouts from the Ganges Valley that are 2500 years old. One image was a drawing published by the Swiss anthropologist Gerhard Baer. He asked a shaman from the Matsigenka tribe in eastern Peru to draw pictures of the places and beings he encountered on his spirit journeys. Among the three figures he drew was one in this posture, with jaguar whiskers to denote its status as a spirit.[43]

The great Feathered Serpent presents herself in varying forms in trance. She may be a snake, a dragon, a centipede, or a great serpentine being who reminds me of the giant worms in Frank Herbert's novel *Dune*. She may also show up as images of curves or spirals that define her undulating body. The lucky trance participants are taken for a ride:

> Stomach hurt. Seemed like Serpent took me in her mouth at my stomach and carried me out into the Void.
>
> I shook as the rattle started moving. It was as though I was riding a fast horse. It was rough, and my body was literally being thrown around. I was breathing hard, and only focus on the rattle kept me upright. Then, after a long time, I was riding on the back of a huge serpent.

The Masked Trance Dance is a remarkable gathering through which the land where the dance takes place is awakened and the animal spirits and other spirits sustaining the natural world are no longer separate from us, the human beings. By entering trance, we join them and invite them to teach us how to participate in recreating the world in a more balanced way. As MaryAnna and I prepared for our first Masked Trance Dance in Ohio, we were nervous, wanting the workshop to go well and wondering if we would remember all the elements of ritual and maskmaking that needed to be woven together. We were also excited, believing that by expanding the work beyond the land of the Cuyamungue Institute, we could bring healing both to the land in Ohio and to the groups of us who live in the area. The hills of southern Ohio were near the places she and I had grown up and lived most of our lives. In February, prior to the dance in July, MaryAnna and I got together to plan and make lists and build the stores of energy we would need for this dance to take place. We chose the Feathered Serpent posture for this early phase of planning because the Feathered Serpent carried within her the life force; therefore, she could be a great help in giving birth to this new phase of our work.

Following are my notes from the trance:

> In the beginning, MaryAnna and I are facing each other, as we actually are, standing across from each other doing this posture. Lines of energy cross in front of us—they are salmon colored. MaryAnna starts hopping and dancing, and so do I. We're really silly, and the voice says, "Frick and Frack do a Trance Dance." Lets me know the spirits don't mind if we lighten up, don't take this Masked Trance Dance too seriously. I see my body as little dots connected by straight lines. The Feathered Serpent moves like many, many little serpentine flows of energy, softening those straight lines. Everything changes from geometric shapes to a rich green jungle, moist and alive. This happens over and over.

The idea was first to align our purpose and energy with the Feathered Serpent. Our light-hearted experience did not mean that we should not

take our work seriously, but was rather a reminder that joy and playfulness are an intrinsic part of interacting with the spirits. Too much seriousness would drain the dance of its power, just as would too much superficiality.

In trance, the Feathered Serpent infused my physical body with her energy, undulating with feminine power, changing geometric and abstract shapes into the verdant living jungle, "moist and alive." This was the feminine and the essence of the Feathered Serpent. Just to make things clear, the experience was repeated, making it impossible for me to miss the point.

When using this posture, people usually enter a womblike place, perhaps a cave or a warm dark environment. After resting there, they rise to a new life. This excerpt from one of my trance experiences shows us that we cannot be attached to who we think we are:

> She [the Feathered Serpent] grates my body on a kitchen grater—I resist then surrender to it. She makes a meatloaf mixture of me—all that is really left is my essence and some meat. [She] shapes me into a baby to begin a new life.

I regularly call upon the Feathered Serpent for help in ritual, especially in creating psychodramas in workshops. Because she leads people into initiatory experiences, the Feathered Serpent posture is ideal for providing the raw material for these ritual dramas. In a Kansas City workshop, the participants created a story from their trance experiences that began with the buffalo, standing alone, bringing into focus for the workshop participants their isolation and longing for the spiritual and community support that was richly woven into the lives of people who lived from the buffalo. As the psychodrama unfolded, however, it became an enactment of a Sun Dance, not exactly a replication of the Lakota Sioux ritual, but with many of the same elements, as verified by two men in the workshop who had participated in a Sun Dance the previous summer.

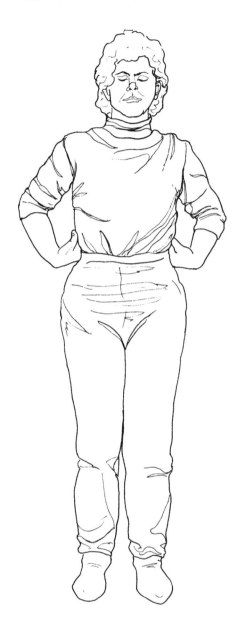

The workshop took place at the spring equinox, traditionally the time when Sun Dancers commit themselves to the months of spiritual preparation for the dance. It was also the time of the budding of new life.

Through the psychodrama, we made personal commitments of gifts and sacrifices so that the people, all the people, might live.

This trance is usually accompanied by a lot of energy and a feeling of renewal. It is rejuvenating, as might be expected from a passage into the darkness of death and night, followed by a rebirth into the freshness of new life.

DESCRIPTION

This is a standing posture. Stand with your feet parallel, about six inches apart, and your toes pointing straight ahead. Keep your knees slightly bent. Cup each hand and place it on the side of your body at the waist. This posture looks like the pose used by children with the song lines, "I'm a little teapot, short and stout, Here is my handle, here is my spout." Curve each arm around to make a "handle." Square your shoulders. Face straight ahead with your eyes closed.

THE GREEK YOUTH AND MAIDEN POSTURE

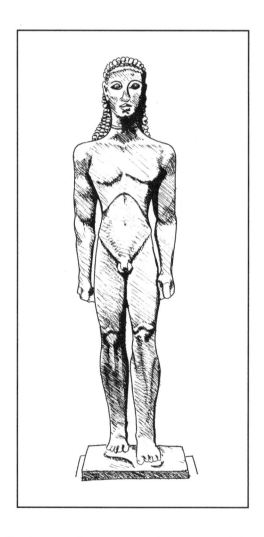

The early Greeks were known to make statues of the male and female versions of this posture and offer them at the shrine at Delphi. The Greeks were not the first to make these figures, however. For hundreds of

years the Egyptians made figures in exactly the same poses before the Greeks adopted them. By the fifth century B.C., however, the details of these statues began to change as the Greeks found themselves in the tran-

sition from horticultural to agricultural society. The details of the posture became less important, giving way to an emphasis on the naturalness of the body and its movements. The changes in the posture reflected the changes in the culture. In the new agricultural society, ecstatic trance using ritual postures disappeared from the spiritual tradition altogether, giving way to theology—reliance more on religious theory than on personal experience.

The trance that is mediated by the two versions of this posture seems to be connected with the Eleusinian Mysteries and the return of Persephone from the Underworld. Nevertheless, of all the postures known to date, this one most links people with the Egyptian deities, which would have been known in the horticultural traditions as spirits rather than gods. In a first experience with this posture, with no hint of its origins, a young woman reported:

> Immediately see an Egyptian cat, light then dark, with compelling blue eyes that pull me into the trance. I am the figure, in porous stone, it seems, just standing. I want to be free and [focus my] will [to make] the stone crumble a little, but then someone is standing close beside me on my left, breathing close to my ear. At first it is just a dark presence, then is the Egyptian jackal god.

Another person commented:

> I became a priestess, saw a cat eye, then a tall dark cat sat beside me. I removed my headdress, which had a crystal in it. The crystal throbbed, and with the sound of it my senses opened up a lot. The headdress became a lyre, and I remembered the Orpheus myth. I understood everything about going to the Underworld with the lyre and bringing back something very beautiful.

The principle expressed in these trances is that of initiation, of dying and being reborn, or of being deprived of integration and then having it restored at a new level. The rituals of the Eleusinian Mysteries often took

place in caves and involved sacrifices of animals, usually piglets that were thrown into crevasses and allowed to rot there, giving off a distinctive odor. Ritual baths in the sea were the usual conclusions to these initiatory celebrations. These elements show up in the trance experiences of people who know nothing about the Eleusinian Mysteries:

> It is dark—night, or deep in a cave or cavern. The drum and rattle sounds are dancers.
>
> Entering a cave with vulva entrance—it is close and bloody and warm and sticky and dark inside.
>
> I swoop into a dark spot like Mammoth Cave—sound of rattle like squealing bats [or squealing piglets?].
>
> Back in time to cave people—prehistoric—very visceral—smell sweat, feel body heat, sounds of gathering and celebration, eating meat.
>
> Looking over a gorgeous azure sea. Slowly rose very high, up into sky as a white bird, diving into the sea and rising up as a woman.

Even for those of us who are not initiates into the Eleusinian Mysteries, there is a longing to understand death and thereby to understand our lives. We desire to know the meaning of being alive in this world. As a therapist, I know the power that comes from telling our stories, from naming who we are and the parts we play in our lives. It is in spiritual practice that we can alter our perspectives so that our lives are brought into context with larger patterns, thus giving larger meanings to our daily experiences. The Greek Youth and Maiden express the marriage of male and female, day and night, life and death. We tend to speak of these mysteries in such ordinary ways. The trance provides the experience by which we can move from one state of being to another, the process through which we can enter the unknown.

DESCRIPTION

Female version: *Stand with your legs straight and your knees locked.*
Keep your feet parallel, close together, with your toes pointing forward. Let
your left arm hang stiffly beside your body, close to your torso, with your fin-
gers held closely together and pointing toward the ground. Place your right
hand on your chest so that the ball of the hand is beneath your right breast and
your fingers are pointing toward your left shoulder. Hold your head erect and

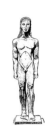

face forward with your eyes closed.

Male version: *Stand with your legs straight and your knees locked, with your left leg extended forward. Position your left foot so that your heel is beside your right toes, and the toes are pointing straight ahead. Place most of your weight on your left leg. Allow your arms to hang straight down, close to your body, your elbows locked. The male statues seem to hold an object in each hand. You can use crystals for this purpose. Close your hands around the crys-*

tals so that your thumbs are on top of your fingers, pointing toward the floor with the thumbnails facing forward. Hold your head erect, and face forward with your eyes closed.

THE LADY OF THESSALY POSTURE

A magnificent figure in this posture was among the hundreds dis-covered by Marija Gimbutas in her archaeological study of goddess figures in pre-patriarchal Europe.[44] Found in the area once known as Thessaly, now Greece, it dates from about 6000 B.C. Its significance as a trance pos-ture is immediately identifiable by the fact that it is a statue of a naked woman wearing a bird mask. In the Neolithic Sesklo culture from which the statue came, the feminine principle was related to the Sun, and women took the form of birds. The masculine principle was related to the Moon, and men took the form of horses. In workshops with the Cuyamungue Institute, we have only used this posture with women, and although we do not know if it is specifically for women, the trances reported are lush with feminine experiences.

Our first encounter with the Lady of Thessaly posture took place at a weekend retreat in the woods of central Ohio. Dr. Goodman beautifully described our introduction to this powerful shamaness spirit in *Where the Spirits Ride the Wind*, in a chapter entitled "In the Land of Centaurs and Mermaids."[45] In that first group of women, we discovered that this posture was a doorway to witnessing the creation of the Earth and experiencing the womb of women as the continually renewing source of that creation. In trance, we experienced an initiation of women in a ritual pool where we died and were reborn, and where women's knowledge of healing and planting was transmitted to the younger ones. Jan's trance revealed some portion of this:

> I found myself sitting in front of a cave that was totally dark behind me, and I was nude. . . . The Moon was out; everything else was very black. . . . I was doing something about contacting (the spirits). . . . It seemed to have something to do with finding out what needed to be done to have a good planting . . . that it was a night of planting. And if the plants were going to grow in the way they needed to, and [produce] a good harvest, then there had to be certain information that was received and acted on.

We all have favorite postures—ones that lead us to experiences that especially nourish us—and this is one of mine. I always feel so voluptuous and refreshed when I use this posture for trance; the Lady of Thessaly also awakens me to what the planet has been and could be, and recommits me to my ecological responsibility. Several years after our introduction to the Lady of Thessaly, I had the following trance:

On the right is a sparkling clean sea, with clean air and sunshine. On the left is the cool darkness of the cave. The clean unpolluted energy is nourishing to our physical bodies. We sit on smooth earth; a beautiful pottery jar is full of clean water. The food is grain, cooked—whole, wholesome. My body is waking up to taking in this unpolluted air, food, water. . . . No place on the planet still has this—we have to go to Alternate Reality to get it. The places I love—like Taos, Lanai—still have a little.

With this experience as the benchmark, my body understands what purity and wholesomeness feel like, and I cannot ignore the environmental issues surrounding me.

At the Cuyamungue Institute, we use this posture when it is time to remember the Earth as a conscious being who has been undergoing her own initiations over the millennia. It draws us into intimate contact with the planet and her children, including ourselves. As women, we are reminded of our sacred trust in being able to bring new life to the world and of the feminine capacity for nurturing all growing things. Through the trance, we learn again how to find our place in the natural order. Men are not excluded from this. Even in the first trance with the Lady of Thessaly posture, Diane tuned into men's roles in the old Thessalonian culture, where the Moon was served by men, and horses were the "children of the Moon" and the bringers of the rains.

I shared this posture with a small group of women who were part of a larger weeklong retreat. As we gathered in the living room of a condominium overlooking the Gulf of Mexico, it seemed appropriate to introduce them to trance through the Lady of Thessaly posture. During trance, the sound of Diane's crying became like background music. Afterward, when we had returned to ordinary consciousness, she told us that as soon as the trance began she was aware of the presence of the old women, and her heart broke and sighed with relief as she felt herself returning to the sisterhood from which she had been apart for lifetimes.

It is that sense of remembering and reunion that characterizes the Lady of Thessaly posture.

DESCRIPTION

Sit on the floor with your knees bent and your legs both extended toward the right. Your feet should be relaxed, with no effort made to point your toes. Tuck your left foot under your right knee. In this position, the weight of your body is primarily on your left buttock. Hold your left arm rigid and place your left hand palm down over your left knee, with the fingers pointing toward a spot about one foot in front of the middle of your body. Your right arm is more relaxed, with your right hand over your right knee, the fingers pointing toward that same midpoint in front of your body. Elongate your neck and turn your head to allow you to look over your right knee.

Maintaining balance in this posture can be difficult, for it puts a strain on the right side of your body. One workshop participant pointed out that few of us have the ample derriere that appears to so comfortably support the woman in the figure. A pillow placed under your left buttock can be used for support.

THE PSYCHOPOMP POSTURE

The Psychopomp is the one who leads the soul, or psyche. In older times, when a person died the shaman or medicine woman would serve as a spiritual guide to lead the soul on its journey to the Realm of the Dead. This is still done in traditional cultures. When we use this posture and make the song or cry that accompanies it, we also become capable of helping the spirits of whose who have died in making their journeys to the Realm of the Dead. It is a very practical way for us to be of service, to give

something back to the spirit realm from which we have received so much learning and healing.

A somewhat modern version of this posture is exhibited by a clay figure from Cochiti Pueblo in New Mexico, dated A.D. 1890. Similar examples of the posture have been located in sub-Saharan Africa. A few years ago a television special by *National Geographic* showed Sudanese women mourning a relative whom the men had gone to bury. They were bewailing the deceased by standing and dancing in this posture, with their hands on their heads. This posture variation, in which people hold their hands on top of their heads instead of above their ears, is also exhibited by an early Greek terra-cotta figure in a brochure for the Joseph Campbell Library at Pacifica Graduate Institute. The female figure is identified as Gaia, the Mother Goddess, with no reference to her unusual posture.

Among the carvings of the Pacific Northwest Native Americans, there is a wonderful example of the Psychopomp posture on a Tsimshian totem pole that stands as a ceremonial entrance to a house. The figure carved in this posture stands above a hole in the totem pole. The hole is an opening between the worlds of the living and the dead, and the shaman in the Psychopomp posture carries the soul of a dead person through that opening.

The first time a group from the Cuyamungue Institute used the posture of the Psychopomp, we knew that our mouths should be open but we did not know that we should make a sound. Jan was the first to realize something was missing: she felt physically uncomfortable and psychically distressed because of the error. She told us at the end of the trance that we should make a sound, and when we did, the emotional tone of the trance changed. In a later use of the Psychopomp posture, when I briefly forgot to make a tone, I felt a heavy pressure inside, and everything around me was dark and swirling. Carol, in another session, said, "I tried to hum, but couldn't. I was dizzy, swaying and struggling. I felt awful."

Why is the sound so important? Over and over again, people report

that the sound creates a bridge, a rope, a tube, or a funnel with which the
spirit of the dead person can make the journey to the Realm of the Dead:

> The sound bridges the abyss.
>
> There was a rope bridge over a deep, deep chasm.
>
> My voice made a sound-tube that opened up like a tunnel with paper
> thin walls that he could walk through.
>
> I saw the circle of us and inside of us was a swirling funnel going up.
>
> I saw Eagle going up a funnel of light. . . . I saw Bear . . . his claws
> were trying to pull someone up into the funnel. . . . Then I saw a transpar-
> ent or translucent figure. I could see the bones, and the body had a red glow.
> It was crawling and climbing up the funnel. There was a hand on the fig-
> ure's shoulder, holding it down. I didn't feel good about the hand and told
> whoever the hand belonged to, to let the figure go.

Apparently some dead people have trouble going over to the other
side, either because they are held back by some force or by living relatives
who do not want to let them go, or because they become lost and don't
know how to find their way. Often, when I have done the Psychopomp
posture for a friend or family member who has died, other spirits also
gather around and follow the first spirit on the journey to the Realm of
the Dead. It is also common to feel the presence of spirits during the
trance. "I felt the circle closed by spirits standing between us," said one
workshop participant. Another commented, "The door to our room
cracked, and I felt a dark presence enter, pass behind me, and then [move]
upward."

All of these elements came together in a trance I experienced for Dr.
Goodman's brother when he died:

> In the beginning I see a chasm from a distance. At first my body is
> very large and I throw it over the chasm, but soon I realize that it is the

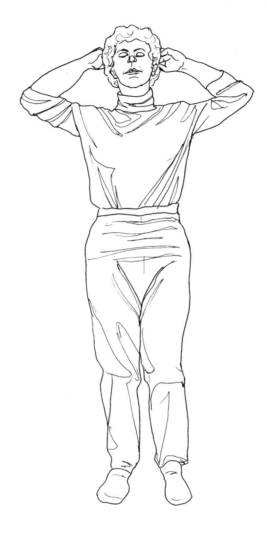

sound that bridges the abyss. Then I am walking across the bridge—sometimes [it is just] ropes and slats, sometimes more substantial. I am holding
his hand in mine, like a little boy's. It is as though I am walking on a higher ground than he is, as though he is shorter. We enter a fog and I say to
just put one foot in front of the other, trusting that the bridge will be there
with each new step. He is afraid, but I tell him to just keep walking through
the cold, gray, wet fog.

Then it is less gray and warmer but still very dense. I see the horns and the head of a white buffalo and say, "Oh, there's Felicitas." He takes her hand and we [all three] walk along until we come to white mountains. I go back to pick up others. There is a rope, which I tell the others they can hold onto to give them direction. . . . We come to a place where the sky is suddenly full of lights—the presence of spirits—welcoming those who have come to cross over. All around is the sound of tinkling rattles, like bells and crickets. I am full of joy, knowing that they will be there when it is time for Felicitas to die, and that they will be there for me one day, too."

DESCRIPTION

The Psychopomp posture could be described as the reverse of the Feathered Serpent posture. Both are standing postures. Place your feet parallel and about six inches apart, your toes pointing forward and your knees kept slightly bent. For the Psychopomp posture, cup your hands and, with your arms raised, fit your fingers just over the top of each ear. Curve your arms around as much as possible, forming "handles" like in the Feathered Serpent posture, with your elbows pointing away from the sides of your body. Hold your mouth open with your jaw relaxed. As the rattling or drumming begins, sound an "Aaah," then allow any other vocalizations that naturally occur during the trance.

Variation: *In the variation of this posture found on the Tsimshian totem pole, the shaman has his mouth closed but is supported on each side by a standing helper. The helper on the left holds his right hand on the back of the shaman's left upper arm at the shoulder; the helper on the right holds his left hand on the front of the shaman's upper right arm at the shoulder. Each helper holds his free arm at his side, raised at the elbow, with the hand gently made into a fist and the palm forward.*

THE VENUS OF LAUSSEL POSTURE

On the cover of a brochure from the Palais des Beaux-Arts in Brussels that advertises an exhibit called "The Human Adventure—5 Million Years," there is a photograph of a woman's figure carved into the side of a cave. She is the Venus of Laussel, and she was carved about 25,000 years ago on the wall of a cave along the Dordogne River near Bordeaux in southern France. In her right hand she holds a bison horn on which there are twelve notches. Her arm is held to her side and raised from the elbow so that her forearm makes a 37-degree angle with her upper arm. As with the other postures of the ancient hunters—such as the Lascaux Cave and the Venus of Galgenberg postures—the 37-degree angle signals a ritual body posture. However, the Venus of Laussel posture is included in the initiation postures instead of the spirit-journey postures because it seems to mediate an initiation into death and a renewal into new life.

The extended left fingers of the Venus point to her navel, the umbilicus that connects her to the Mother. Many reports from people who have used this posture include words like "dissolving," "fecundity," and "renewal":

> There was a circle of people lying on the floor, around a central fire. Around a swirling flame images emerged, then melted and dissolved into the next image. I experienced my body dissolving.

> There was a large, fat, Grandmother Spider, laughing and ancient. She had hundreds of little black spiders she could command. The Venus was connected spiritually with Grandmother Spider.

> I saw a young woman who was myself in a grass skirt rimmed in flowers, dancing the hula . . . dancing to bring the seed. Then the seed was inside me and I was dancing. I had received the other into my body and was nourishing something neither it or me but both.

> There was a dance with swirling skirts that turned into nice, happy snakes with their tongues flickering. . . . Big snakes began eating the tiny little snakes until they got bigger and slower, and finally they were just one big snake.

The spider is a powerful figure in other traditions, because she is able to create material substance from her own body. Snakes in many cultures

are representative of tranformation, since they are able to renew themselves by shedding their skins. The uroborus, the snake biting its tail, has
long been a symbol for the renewal of life.

In one workshop, this experience of life recreating itself was told
through me:

I rose on the wind, ever so gently out of my body, floating. Then I became the Venus carved of rock, huge and getting bigger, towering over the landscape. I felt as though I participated in the feminine spirit of the Earth, felt her fresh and young. The Earth was rich brown and green, fresh and clean. . . . I felt myself on the cave wall—my body was the carving—felt we can all participate in the Earth's renewal through our own bodies and our own lives. Aware of my belly, my fecundity, the capacity for renewal through new life. Aware of the horn—it became more phallic. They come together to create new life—life recreating herself, remember? She [the Venus] reminded me that I knew this all along.

The full meaning of the bison horn is not clear. It may be a crescent moon, signifying the maiden and the beginning of the moon cycle. Its twelve notches may divide a year into thirteen moons. It may represent a cornucopia, a horn of plenty. Eventually experience, and the Venus of Laussel herself, will tell.

DESCRIPTION

This is a standing posture in which your legs are close together with your knees locked, your feet parallel, and your toes pointing forward. Your right hand holds a crescent-shaped bison horn, which you can replicate using a cardboard cutout. Hold the fingers of your right hand close together. The crescent is held between your fingers and thumb, with your fingers facing forward. Hold your right arm to the side of your body, bent at the elbow, with the crescent raised to shoulder level. The angle between your upper arm and lower arm should be 37 degrees. Hold your left arm close to your body and place your left hand on your abdomen above your navel, angled so the first two fingers of your left hand are pointing toward your navel. Spread your fingers. Face toward the left with your eyes closed.

Living Myths

Time is simply a construct that we use to give structure and order to our existence. Time as we know it is not a condition that defines Alternate Reality. In part, this means that there is no past or future, but that everything coexists at the same time. What we know as historical events are still taking place somewhere in time, and we can locate those events and participate in them as they are occurring. In Richard Bach's book *Illusions*, he likens events in time to scenes on a movie reel.[46] The scenes or events of the movie continue to exist over time, wound up on the reel. At any chosen time, it is possible to "play" them in our consciousness, which, like a projector, brings them to life for us. However, there is a difference in Alternate Reality in that we can become participants in those events, not just observers.

To some people, this sounds pretty weird. I think it is not so different from what we experience in dreams. I may dream of an old friend from high school and revisit places and people from that time in my life. However, what I feel and how I react in the dream may be different from my recollection of that period in my life. I bring to the dream consciousness the developmental changes and new awareness I have acquired over the past thirty years. Nevertheless, the dream is part of my reality, and I can go back in time without losing my ordinary consciousness.

The three postures in this chapter on living myths give us the opportunity to go back into time that is not part of personal memory but belongs to the archives of other cultures. These postures take us into stories that have become myths in those cultures. The postures were most likely gifts to the people of those societies that allowed them to take part in their cultural myths. Through trance, the myths are personally experienced with freshness and focus, rather than becoming stale with retelling over time. Consider what it would be like to enter the ecstatic trance state and visit the life of Christ, witnessing, for instance the Sermon on the Mount and the changing of stones into fish, and water into wine. Each of us might see or feel something uniquely personal, yet we would share something in common. And undoubtedly we would respond to the stories differently from hearing them read or told 2000 years later.

Because the myths revisited in the living myths postures do not belong to the cultural heritage of many workshop participants, they may not mean as much to these participants as they would to those who heard the stories from their grandmothers and grandfathers. These postures are included in the workshops, nevertheless, as opportunities for participants to understand how myths can be living events and as ways for them to appreciate myths from traditions other than their own.

The Emergence posture shares a story from the People who were the ancestors of the Pueblo and Navajo Indians. It is the story of an exodus up to the Earth above from the Third World (or Fourth World, depending on where the story is told), which exists below the world as we know it. The emergence into the Fourth World or Fifth World was necessitated by conditions of chaos and misery. These conditions are experienced in the trance. The Man of Cuautla posture returns us to a Mayan myth from the *Popol Vuh*. This myth arose during a time when the culture was making a transition from horticulture to agriculture and the Quiche Mayan people were given patron deities from the new gods. The Mayan Whistle posture invites us to participate in the story of a warrior's death and his journey to the afterlife.

At the Cuyamungue Institute, when we originally worked with the Greek Youth and Maiden and Lady of Thessaly postures, we included them in the category of living myths. However, our continuing experiences have suggested that while these two ritual postures mediate trances linked with cultural myths, they also provide experiences that personally engage us in initiations. In the trances mediated by these postures, we are not observers of unfamiliar ceremonies but participants who are meaningfully involved, coming away with understandings that change our lives. The boundary dividing the categories of living myth postures and initiation postures may be artificial. The postures of each group may lie along a continuum between the poles of cultural and personal experience. Each posture offers, to varying degrees, the possibility of an inner awakening as well as an appreciation of the culture from which it came.

THE EMERGENCE POSTURE

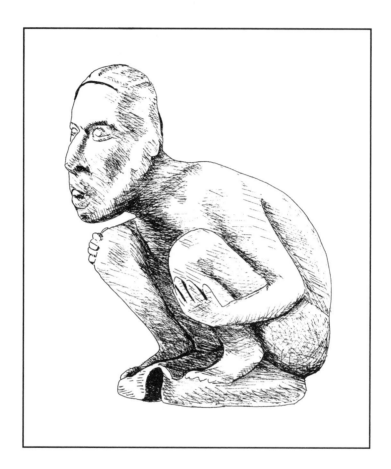

A figure of a man squatting in this position is on the end of a carved redstone pipe found in Hale County, Alabama. It dates from around A.D. 1300, approximately the same date the Tennessee Diviner was carved from stone in nearby Tennessee. The people who carved these figures were linked with the Maya and perhaps with the Anasazi, so it makes sense to associate the experiences in this posture with the emergence stories of the

Pueblo Indians, and their neighbors the Navajo. Another figure in this posture is carved in green stone and has the elongated face characteristic of the Olmecs.

The Pueblo myth of the beginning is told by Alphonso Ortiz in *The Tewa World*.[47] The Tewa are a branch of the northern Pueblo people, today comprising six of eight pueblos.

> The Tewa were living in Sipofene beneath Sandy Place Lake far to the north. The world under the lake was like this one, but it was dark. Supernaturals, men, and animals lived together at this time, and death was unknown. Among the supernaturals were the first mothers of all the Tewa, known as "Blue Corn Woman" . . . and "White Corn Maiden." These mothers asked one of the men present to go forth and explore the way by which the people might leave the lake. Three times the man refused, but on the fourth request he agreed. He went out first to the north, but saw only mist and haze; then he went successively to the west, south, and east, but again saw only mist and haze. . . . Next the mothers told him to go to the above.

The man returned to report that this Earth seemed inhabitable, and the People are said to have emerged from a lake in the Jemez Mountains in north-central New Mexico.

There is a related Navajo story about Coyote, the grand old trickster who was always causing trouble. Even though he would play practical jokes and generally annoy everyone, he was usually the one who suffered the most from his own pranks. However, for all his mischief, he was the son of Mother Earth and Father Sky, and was thus the bridge between the two realities. For the millionth time, Coyote was doing something he shouldn't have, and as a result caused flood waters to rise in the Fourth World. The humans who lived there were forced to flee and thus emerged in the Fifth World, our Earth, for safety.

Neither of these emergence stories portrays the terrifying conditions reported by people who use the Emergence posture for trance. They tell of the chaos and misery that necessitated the migration to the Earth. They often experience darkness and a violent world in turmoil. In trance, they witness the moaning and screaming of those who are about to die, or they briefly become one of those who is struggling to get to the other world; some succeed and some die. Not surprisingly, this misery, along with the general awkwardness of the position, make it one of the most unpopular postures.

Following is the account of my first experience using the Emergence posture:

Pain shoots across my back. I hear the sound of rattlesnakes; they are upset and sounding a warning. There are thousands of them. The Earth is cracked and parched and I see mountains in the distance. There is rumbling in the ground and thunder. I heard what sounds like a smoke alarm. Then a George Washington figure emerges from the ground, followed by lots of people covered in stinking mud. I eat a lizard and it makes me throw up. Is there any food?

Judy, who was in trance beside me, saw her Eagle friend. She was aware of my discomfort and surrounded me with energy, like an egg. Her impression was that it was necessary for me to break out of the shell of the egg. Both of us experienced a pressure to break through something, to become free and emerge into different conditions.

DESCRIPTION

Stand with your feet apart and lower your body into a squatting position, bringing your torso forward so that it bends over your knees. Keep the heels of your feet close to the floor. If you have a less-than-perfectly limber body and cannot actually sit in a squatting position with your buttocks on the ground like the man in the figurine, you can pile up pillows to form a stool. The weight of your body is still mostly on your feet, but the pillows help with balance.

Place your left hand on your lower left leg, with the ball of your hand just below your knee and your fingers pointing up toward your kneecap. Rest your right hand palm down on the outer edge of your right knee, with your arm held close to the side of your leg. Face forward with your eyes closed.

The small carved figure from Alabama wears a cap made of strips of cloth or hide. We have not replicated his hat at the Cuyamungue Institute, even though it is probably significant since it is the only thing he is wearing.

THE MAN OF CUAUTLA POSTURE

The little clay sculpture of a man in this posture has an elaborate headdress and neckpiece. The statue belongs to a Swiss woman named Ursula who is a student and friend of Dr. Goodman. Her uncle had emigrated from Switzerland to Mexico City, and when his house was being built there, the construction crew unearthed this statue. He gave it to his mother, Ursula's grandmother, who later bequeathed it to her. Ursula's trance experience while she was using this posture helped clarify its purpose, which is to provide an opening into a mythical event from the Mayan religious tradition.

There is a story in the *Popol Vuh*[48] of a time in the history of the Quiché Mayan people when agriculture was beginning to take over from horticulture as the dominant way of life. During this major time of transition, new spirits arrived: evil white spirits who murdered the people who would not worship them. New people were made of cornmeal, and the heads of families were required to go to Tulan Zuyua, the seven caves, to obtain new patron deities from the reigning spirits. Even today, beneath the Pyramid of the Sun at Teotihuacan, there is a natural cave with seven chambers, suggesting that the mythical story recounted in the *Popol Vuh* may have some connection to events in ordinary reality.

In trance, Ursula was guided down stone steps deep into the Earth until she "arrived in a large hall with a domed ceiling." Stone frogs and stone snakes "all wanted to get out" and were freed by traveling back up the stone steps. Her guide on the journey was a shadow, with "a red spot in the middle of its chest, which glowed and rotated." It is relevant to note that the Mayan god Tohil was in charge of the dispensation of new gods to the Quiché people. Tohil was often represented with a smoking mirror on his forehead or a glowing red fire on his chest.

At the beginning of this trance, it is common to feel a whirling or twirling, combined with movement down into something. Some people see a tunnel or water, or experience going underground or into a cave. Judith, for instance, reported:

> I become a snake, and within my body are rooms. We all go inside
> the snake and go through the various rooms until we find an opening that
> takes us below. We go far into the lower earth.

There, like Ursula, she found snake people "who have much to tell us about the Earth's destruction." This is not surprising considering the

destruction of the Quiché culture and the struggle of the people to survive under new gods.

In the same group doing the Man of Cuautla posture, Nancy said that the posture hurt her body so much that she could not remain in it for fifteen minutes. Judy felt so much energy that she thought she would burst out of her body. For her, the Earth was spinning, and she saw everything upside down.

Sometimes in trance we witness events that are relevant to a particular culture, but it is hard to tell whether they represent a personal story or belong to the collective. Without access to a global compendium of myths ranging from the dawn of consciousness to the present time, we cannot easily track down the stories from our excursions into Alternate Reality. An example is the following Man of Cuautla trance told by Jackie. After being picked up by a bumblebee, she is dropped into the stem of a flower:

> [I come out] "in lava, then see a scene of flat slabs of rock and a sycamore tree. A panther (black) comes along, stretches, scratches bark of tree, then jumps to an inviting limb. Watches as a tribe of Indians dance around fire on the flat rocks. The panther jumps into fire [like a sacrifice] and burns and melts. Indians rub its ashes on their faces and leave. Spirit of panther jumps back into tree and watches. Then it flies into sky and dances with other animal spirits and then returns to the tree. It is night during all of this. The Moon seems to be crying but it's a peaceful feeling. The eyes of the panther remain in the fire pit, the sky, and the tree. Felt I could hear the panther breathing throughout the trance.

Jackie's trance experience has the beauty of a mythical story. For now, we can only store it away in memory, waiting for a serendipitous moment when someone trips over an obscure myth that will tell the story she saw in trance with the Man of Cuautla.

DESCRIPTION

Sit on the floor with your legs stretched out straight ahead. Then bend your knees slightly and raise them from the floor so that only your heels and buttocks remain on the floor. Spread your knees so that your thighs form a "V". Keep your heels on the floor about six inches apart. Cup your right hand and place it palm down over your right kneecap. Cup your left hand and place it just to the left side of your left kneecap. Bend your elbows and hold your arms fairly close to your body. Let your tongue rest on your upper teeth and protrude from between your lips. Face forward, with your eyes closed.

THE MAYAN WHISTLE POSTURE

Unearthed from tomb number 23 at the Rio Azul diggings in Guatemala, one stern little figure in this posture is a whistle. It is hollow and makes a whistling sound when you blow into its upper opening. Warrior figures sitting in this posture were also discovered at the classical Mayan site at Jaina on the western side of the Yucatan peninsula, but they were not whistles. Our experience at the Cuyamungue Institute with other whistling vessels leads us to believe that, historically, the whistling sound was used along with the posture to promote trance and hence facilitate the reliving of a mythic event.

The Mayan whistle was placed in a grave, perhaps as a reminder of the myths of the afterlife and assurances that immortality could be stolen from the Lords of Death. From early trance experiences with the Mayan Whistle posture, Dr. Goodman speculates that it reveals the story of a warrior's death and his journey to the afterlife, including all the trials that must be faced when the soul departs from the body after death. In *Where the Spirits Ride the Wind*,[49] Dr. Goodman fits together fragments from trances and wraps them with her own intuitions to tell the story of such a warrior's journey. The story is entitled "A Ghost Says Goodbye." Since he is from the Mayan culture, it is likely that the warrior is preparing for the trials of the underworld Xibalba, where he will face the same challenges that the Hero Twins Hunahpu and Xbalanque faced with the Lords of Death. If he is successful, he will be free of death and dance to the North Star. If he fails, he will rot in the Underworld.

In our own trances at the Cuyamungue Institute, one detail of the posture made a significant difference in the nature of the experience. In my most recent trance using the Mayan Whistle posture, I found myself sitting on a ledge overlooking a snow-covered plain where a steam-powered locomotive chugged its way toward the mountains in the distance. I sat "like a sphinx" while all around me was nothing but the wind and the cold and blowing sand. I was immovable. It reminded me of my very first time using this posture, when I described myself feeling "like stone, very cold, and slow, slow energy. I was just sitting there with the desert wind blowing over me." At that moment, something prompted me to pay attention to my body's positioning, and I realized that my thumbs were sticking out. I quickly tucked them under each armpit and the character of the trance immediately brightened. Now the train moved through a green cornfield ripe with yellow ears, while I sat in the field enjoying the warmth of the sunny sky:

I focused in my body, feeling like a warrior—all instinct, reactive, with little self-reflection or empathy, only a focus on my goal, getting what I wanted. There was the scent of flowers, like gardenias, and the softness of a woman.

Later, in rereading Dr. Goodman's chapter on the Mayan Whistle, I came upon her memory of a moment when the "room of the university building was filled with the intoxicating fragrance of the blossoms of a jasminelike bush the villagers call 'Juan de noche,'" which she associated with a funeral procession. Maybe the sweet smell of flowers I had noticed was the same fragrance.

During my trance, I believed that promises had been made to us warriors to engage our loyalty and fierceness. At the same time, Judy was in trance flying with Eagle. Then she was "grounded like a funnel to the Earth." The funnel was like a column of energy, and at the base of the column she found diamonds. She went to the center of the Earth, then flew high again, then went back to the molten core. Finally she saw a huge egg about to explode, and there was lots of light.

I speculated about how Judy's trance could have been related to the story of a warrior's journey in the afterlife. She flew with her longtime spirit friend, Eagle, the one who flies between Earth and sky, connecting the two worlds. Each time she flew freely, she was afterward brought deep into the Earth. This may have been her experience of going into the Lower World. This was not horrible like the terrible tasks the Lords of Death in Xibalba might have had in store for the warrior, but she did have an experience each time she entered the Earth. Briefly she flew free, then she returned for another task.

At the end of Judy's trance, the egg exploded. In some traditions, the energy fields that surround the body of a person are likened to an egg, called an auric egg in Western metaphysics. It would make sense that when the final tasks in Xibalba are completed, the soul is released from its shell, the limits that contain and define the human being. The soul can then explode into light as it dances toward its new home in the Milky Way.

DESCRIPTION

Sit cross-legged on the floor, with your left leg in front of your right leg and your left foot tucked under your right knee. Cross your arms over the front of your chest, with your left arm on top of your right one. Tuck your left hand into your right armpit. With your right hand, hold onto the left side of the body just below your armpit. Be sure to keep your thumbs tucked under your armpits. Hold your upper arms rigid, with your elbows pointing forward, away from your body at about a 45-degree angle. Face straight ahead, your eyes closed, and your tongue protruding from between your lips.

Celebration

The word *celebration* comes from the Latin verb *celebratus*, meaning "to frequent." Celebration has various meanings: to perform a ceremony publicly; to honor by solemn ceremony; to hold up for public notice; to demonstrate satisfaction with festivities; to make merry. I looked up the word to try to understand why Dr. Goodman had intuitively chosen it to identify the Calling the Spirits and Singing Shaman postures. At one level, this decision is undoubtedly related to our custom of using the Calling the Spirits posture to invite spirits to join us when we celebrate a Masked Trance Dance. Having made masks and costumes to honor the animal spirits whom we have met in our journeys to the Lower World, we invite them, through this posture, to inhabit the masks and join in the festivities of the ritual, as well as the dance and feast that follow. We may also invite these beings who live in Alternate Reality to join us at the beginning of a new undertaking, like the beginning of a writing project or the creation of a new medicine wheel. We are honoring these events with the inclusion of these special guests, and perhaps we are even "making the events public" in Alternate Reality by doing so.

The "celebration" behind the Singing Shaman posture is a little less clear. It is a favorite posture for newcomers. As they stand in a circle, or even in an auditorium, all who are participating can hear the gradual transition of the entire group into the trance state. The initial hum of a chorus of "aaaahhh" sounds is replaced by harmonious or discordant voices, some deep and others rising into higher octaves, some sounding like animal noises and others falling into the distinctive rhythm and intonation of glossolalia.

Often, when the rattling ends, there is a final a cappella conclusion that would make any choir director proud. Because it is beautiful and easily shared among a group, this is a good posture to introduce people to ecstatic trance. It is an easy posture. The sound of one's own voice, as well as the sound of other voices, gives a person something on which to focus, in addition to the rattling. Concentration is a key to helping people learn to shift into the trance state. The auditory input also offers a distraction from the mental chatter newcomers usually experience—the line of questions asking, "What's going on?" and "Am I doing what I'm supposed to?" and "Is this really a trance?" and "I must be must making this up."

Many times people really enjoy the Singing Shaman posture. The singing is often very joyful and accompanied by witnessing or being part of dancing and, indeed, celebration. There is more to the Singing Shaman posture than this, however. It offers a very powerful trance experience in which a connection is made with some realm of Alternate Reality. It may be an experience of crying to the star people for a vision, or giving voice to the pain of Mother Earth or her children. It may be creating a channel with the sound vibrations of one's voice, allowing a tangible connection to be made between ordinary and nonordinary realities. There is a power in this posture that is not to be taken lightly.

The Latin verb *celebratus* means "to frequent." Sometimes we make decisions and choose words without consciously understanding their full import. We may "frequent" a place, visiting it often, making a habit of going there. Over time, a relationship develops with the place, as well as with the people, things, plants, animals that belong in that place. Perhaps these two postures help us establish relationships with the spirits through the celebration of ritual: the ritual of the trance itself, as well as other rituals that bring the spirits into our lives in ordinary reality.

Dr. Goodman writes about the postures as rituals, each one a complete ritual within itself. In her own words, she describes the importance of body posture in achieving the experience of ecstatic trance:

> To attempt to define "religion" is a futile undertaking. It is more use-
> ful instead to state what religion does—what the purpose of activity consid-

ered to be religious by the participants aims to do. And that is as follows: All human societies endeavor to take up contact with powers or beings of the "other," sacred reality. This is the purpose of all religious rituals, but these rituals are not the same in all societies or faiths. It was my discovery that very ancient types of societies, the hunter-gatherers, and principally the horticulturalists, a type of society that antedates agriculture, possessed, and in part still possess today, a special type of ritual. In a nutshell, this ritual, which is of great sophistication, consists of assuming certain highly specific body postures, and then of achieving contact with the sacred reality by rhythmically stimulating the body. The postures mediate the experience, [and] the rhythmic stimulation adds the biological component, the bodily door, as it were, without which this type of religious experience is not possible. Because the ritual consists of only the body posture cum stimulation, and does not carry any other cultural baggage, such as specific music, songs, prayers, and so on, this valuable experience is accessible to anyone.[50]

Therefore, the trance relates to the physiological changes that take place when we do something to the body like fast, use hallucinogenic drugs, or arouse the nervous system by rattling or drumming. Ecstatic trance also requires a ritual. The trance gets us to Alternate Reality, but the ritual affects how we perceive that reality. There are many different rituals used by various cultures for this purpose. The postures are, in themselves, complete rituals. They provide rituals so powerful that no cultural context is required to accomplish their purpose. So, we are able to accomplish a Calling of the Spirits ritual with only rattling and a posture used by the Olmec people hundreds of years ago.

One of the disheartening realities of being city dwellers is that our cultural lifestyle is generally devoid of rituals that bring us into connection with the sacred. Realizing this void, sensitive and spiritually inclined people are focusing their attention on remedying the situation. There are a number of books and some workshops that draw upon the vast range of cultural traditions of creating rituals. One thing that characterizes us city dwellers, to our benefit I believe, is our capacity to integrate varying traditions. We have an inherent ability to weave related practices from different sources into new forms that are stronger. This is an organic process of change that has always existed. Not all new forms are stronger, of course. Some people try to take elements of traditions about which they have no understanding, and they miss the import and intention of the rituals. Others may attempt to adopt the practices of other cultures without recognizing that our own cultural traditions are very much part of who we are.

Most of us are people who live in an urban culture. But we can "apply these shamanic practices to the needs of people living in the dominant culture."[51] We can learn from those who know the path of the spirits better than we do. We can adopt the postures as rituals that have been handed down to us and that do not require a prescribed dogma or cultural context. And we must be respectful of the spirits and their world, to which we have been granted entrance.

It is good for all of us to come to the celebration postures with humility and joy, asking that the spirits join us and that we learn to help in creating the connections between our world and the world of the spirits.

THE CALLING THE SPIRITS POSTURE

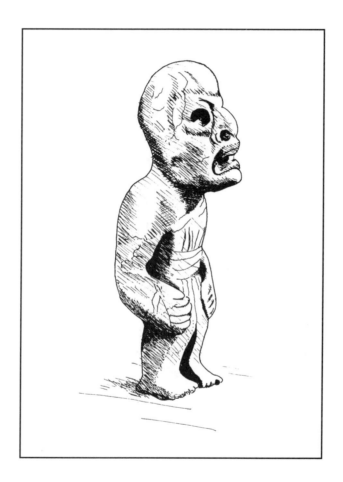

A small clay figure stands in this posture, his elongated head and long jaw line characteristic of the statues of the Olmec people. His mouth hangs open. His hands, which are the keys to this ritual posture, are spread into the seams of his body at the groin. When I stretch my own fingers to find their places in the powerful region of the pelvis, knowing that in ritual this intimate gesture is respected, my body stands a little taller, even before the rattling begins.

Dr. Goodman tells the story in *Where the Spirits Ride the Wind* of her first contact with this little man.[52] As a visiting lecturer for the School of American Research in Santa Fe, she was taken on a private tour of their museum. She stopped before a little yellowish clay statue, about 5½ inches tall, which was standing on a pedestal clearly labeled "Calling the Spirits." The posture intrigued her, and right away, upon returning home, she tried it with a group of coworkers at the Cuyamungue Institute. It was not until the next year, however, that she thought to add a slide of this statue to her collection. By then, however, no one at the School of American Research had ever seen or heard of the little man, and his place on the shelf was inhabited by a larger, prone figure. Dr. Goodman insisted, but no evidence of this figure could be identified, even when she reviewed the slides of the museum's entire collection. Maybe this experience was a tease, a trick played by the spirits, a wandering across that line between ordinary and nonordinary reality.

The Olmec figurine I always see when I think of this posture is the one displayed in the National Museum of Anthropology in Mexico City. He stands only 2½ inches tall and looks strikingly similar to other Olmec figures and drawings. These figures are so familiar to me that it is hard to remember that the Olmecs were a mysterious people about whom very little is known. One day when I asked Dr. Goodman for suggestions of books to read about the Olmecs, she smiled and said, "There is very little written. We probably know more about them than all the archaeologists and anthropologists put together, because we know them from having shared in their ritual and in their spirit world."

It is known that the Olmec people lived on the Gulf Coast plain of Mexico about 3000 years ago. Their name, *Olmec*, means "men of rubber," referring to their discovery of latex, which they used to make rubber boots and rubber balls. Their ritual ball games, played by priests, were

similar to those played in the grand plazas of the Mayan and Aztec people, who lived in the same region centuries later. The Olmec society was organized into city-states, loosely joined by trade and a common culture. Their language, which was proto-Mayan, was not preserved in written form, but they left evidence of themselves in rock drawings and clay figurines. Several important postures are from the Olmecs.

The Calling the Spirits posture was not specific to the Olmecs, however. There is a beautiful carving from the Pacific Northwest of a woman lying on the back of a dogfish, her hands in the characteristic position of this posture. The woodcarver obviously knew the experience of trance, since the woman's eyes convey that unmistakable inner gaze so well known to those who have made trance journeys. One warm afternoon in May, while sitting in her living room, I asked Dr. Goodman to tell me the story of the woman being carried away by the dogfish. There was no written story, she told me, but it was sometimes suggested that the woman was being carried off as punishment for something she had done wrong. That kind of thinking smacked of missionary attitudes but was not consistent with the pre-Christian traditions of the Pacific Northwest Indians. I knew by the look in her eyes that Dr. Goodman had more thoughts on the matter. Careful to remind me that her comments were only speculations, she raised the question of why this story might have been suppressed. It was commonly known that stories and information not consistent with missionary theology were destroyed or altered so that their meanings would not be preserved. Perhaps the woman was an apprentice who, by calling upon the dogfish and entering trance, was being taken to a realm in Alternate Reality where the spirits associated with her people resided. Or she may have called upon the dogfish to help her escape mistreatment at the hands of a father or husband. There was abuse in those cultures, too, Dr. Goodman said, and the remedy may have been provided by the spirit world.

The Calling the Spirits posture is usually done as an invitation to those in the world of spirits. It calls them to join in a gathering or a celebration. At the Cuyamungue Institute, it is a traditional part of our Masked Trance Dance to call the spirits on the afternoon prior to the dance, asking them to come to the kiva or other sacred space where we have gathered, and inviting them to inhabit the masks we have created for them. If we are at the Institute itself, this ceremony takes place in the kiva, where the masks are hung on the circular walls while we experience the trance. One participant described how she saw the spirits responding to the call:

> First I saw the lioness mask, then the lioness herself. She and her mate entered the kiva; she sat on my left and he was on my right. Then I saw the crow mask [Johanna] and the deer [Judy]. I realized that all the spirits had come to join us. The kiva was full of spirits. Then I saw that we were all gathered around a fire on an open plain, with a mountain in the distance. There was an even greater congregation of spirits around the fire. Those who were the spirits of the masks stood beside us and we waited for the sunrise to begin the dance. We were fed with a rich royal jelly from the Bee People. I had a feeling of being made whole, that for a brief time each cell was made perfect. Later we all danced and sang together.

In another trance, it was made clear that when we invite the spirits to become part of a project, the energy that feeds the project comes from resources deeper than an individual person can provide.

> I see a tree with its roots wrapped around my breast. . . . Then a deep root goes into my breast and through my heart, down to wrap itself around my uterus and then deep into the Earth. When it taps the Earth, my fear for my breast vanishes and the tree becomes healthy. It is not a danger so long as it draws its life force from the Earth and not me. With this realization, my body develops a thick healthy bark and I feel well grounded.

Often, in this posture, people either see tall poles or trees, or more commonly, they experience becoming trees. Sometimes the tree image is clear. Other times it is only suggested. A person may grow very, very tall, swaying in the winds of the sky. Energy may focus on the top of the head, which seems to sprout and grow tall. Or a person may become solid and rough and begin to grow deep roots into the body of the Earth. Carol described becoming a tree in the following way:

> I saw a great yellow ball of Sun with spirals coming off. Then Eagle appeared on the Sun, and then a great tree with Sun behind. . . . And then I was a flash of soft, yet penetrating milk-white light that went up the center of the trunk of the tree. As I was in tree, or was tree, I saw Eagle and Wolf in several forms, and always in the midst of the forms was a face of an elder.

This tree is the Tree of the World, reaching up into the Sky World, where the ancestors live and where the essential patterns of all creation reside. This tree also stands solid and firm in the Middle World of ordinary consciousness, and penetrates the Lower World, which is home to the animal spirits and the Realm of the Dead. In one trance, when MaryAnna called the spirits, Owl, Eagle, Hawk, and Raven came to her. As the bird spirits are the emissaries of the Sky World, MaryAnna knew that on that occasion she was answered by the spirits of the upper branches of the Tree.

Another workshop participant, a newcomer experiencing her very first trance, was visited by family members, her dog, and her dead parents, all responding from the Middle World and the Realm of the Dead in the Lower World. It is not unusual for the spirits to visit us in the forms we are best able to see and welcome. A gathering of animal spirits may come from the Lower World, especially when we invite them to the Masked Trance Dance. Singing and dancing are often part of these

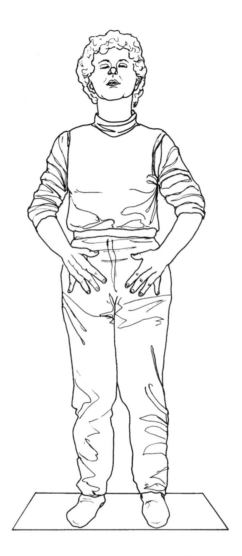

celebrations in Alternate Reality before we actually begin the dance in this world, and singing and dancing are often included in ordinary reality when we invite the spirits to join us.

Recently, Judy called the spirits with an intention of studying the meaning of this posture. She saw the famous mammoth statues of Easter Island and a small fire-being dancing between the huge stone gods. She later wrote, "I alternated between being the statue and the dancer." The message she understood was that this posture can be used to bridge the duality of ancient and contemporary life. Just a week later, in a Calling the Spirits trance, I began hearing a chorus of soprano voices coming from the stars, the Sky World. Later there was a bass chorus, deep and brown and of the Earth. The message came: "Bridge them." Did this mean that the Calling the Spirits posture is to be used for bridging? It seems that it can be, but it is good to be cautious about defining the purpose of a posture too narrowly.

Especially when this posture is used to call the spirits to the masks, or for other very particular purposes, the experiences can be similar to metamorphosis trances. People often describe gatherings of animal faces, or the presence of special animal spirit friends. However, no one actually becomes an animal, which is the primary characteristic of metamorphosis trance. Other times, there is an inner experience of crying out, of "mouths wailing," which is more like the other celebration posture, the Singing Shaman.

DESCRIPTION

This is one of the standing postures. Stand with your feet parallel, about six inches apart, and your toes directed straight ahead. Keep your knees slightly bent to prevent a strain on your lower back. Spread the fingers of each hand as wide as possible. Position the middle finger of each hand in the crease where your leg joins your torso, with your other fingers lying against your body. Hold your upper arms stiff and away from your body. With your eyes closed, tip your head back slightly. Keep your mouth open during the trance, as though you are calling out, but do not make any sound.

THE SINGING SHAMAN POSTURE

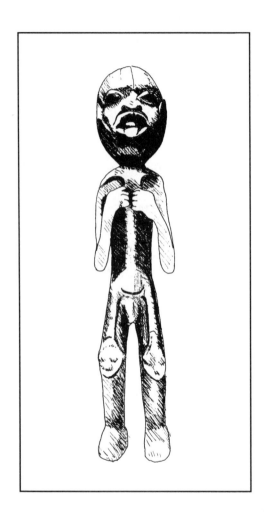

Carved figures in the Singing Shaman posture have been identified in a wide range of geographic locales, from Melanesia and New Guinea to Alaska and Central America. The oldest is from the Cyclades Islands, in Greece, and is about 5000 years old.

The Singing Shaman posture is one of only two postures in which a sound is intentionally made throughout the trance. The singing affects people deeply, both emotionally and physically. Often people in workshops speak about their feelings of oneness and wholeness as they participate in the harmony of voices. One woman spoke of weaving a basket with the sounds. Another said the voices were "all different, yet all one." Others said, "I can't separate me from the sound," and "I feel a wholeness and completeness with all who have ever done this posture."

It is not unusual for people doing this posture to have the feeling of losing control over their voices. Nancy described having one note in mind, but her intention was not related to what came out of her mouth. She experienced a paradox of feeling as though she could sing forever, yet believing she couldn't keep it going another minute. John heard a vibrato arising from his own throat, an unintended sound coming as though from a tube, with no intellectual control on his part. The voice was ancient, and it was as though he had heard it singing many times before. Many people experience hearing ceremonial chanting or animal noises coming out of their throats. At times, the kiva is filled with the sounds of bears growling or coyotes yelping at the moon. The dogs who live at the Cuyamungue Institute may even take up the song outside.

For some people, this lack of control creates a sense of freedom, of being free to sing out loud, to let their voices be heard. One person confessed her delight at finally having permission to make a sound in front of someone. As she heard her own voice with the others, Ann told herself in the trance that she "should get in union" with the other voices, but immediately she heard the message, "No, let it happen." She later said, "I wanted, even needed to be off-key, in disharmony. I started wailing, then heard someone else wailing and went into a huge grief process." She experienced a release and relief from some of the grief she had carried over the death of her mother the previous year.

In almost every group, someone will become attuned to personal grief or the pain of the Earth herself. Elizabeth felt, in trance, that "the whole world groans in travail," and Janet heard "Mother Earth crying about what we have done" to her. After the trance, the workshop leader may ask specifically if someone had a trance that was sad or painful. Sometimes those who felt grief or heard crying have quietly decided that their experience would detract from the joyfulness of others. However, they hold a necessary awareness that keeps everyone grounded and in balance, and they are encouraged to share. Those who carry the grief may need the loving support of the group, and those who are joyful have the opportunity to embrace their counterparts.

Again and again, people who have done this posture speak of feeling as though the sound of the singing opens their hearts and throats. Once in an introductory workshop, I instructed the group to use the wrong hand position for the Singing Shaman posture, telling the people to touch their forefingers instead of their little fingers. Because of the error, I learned from a nurse in the group that the little fingers are neurologically connected with the heart, so the positioning of the hands in the Singing Shaman posture allows the energy or feelings of the heart to pour out from the throat.

While this is not specifically a healing posture, many people report positive physical changes. All of the standing postures facilitate drawing the energy from the Earth's surface up through the body. Aided by the vibration of sounds, the physical sensations created in this trance can be profound. Wyn said she could feel the vibration in her knee, which was still healing from a recent surgery.

About eight years ago, I received a message about healing during a Singing Shaman trance:

> My spirit flew up out of my body toward the Sun. As I got away from
> the Earth, I looked back and my heart melted at the beauty of it. There was
> an intense light at the center, and if I sang very high I could go to the cen-

ter and sound the note of the planet and its vibrations. From within the Earth I could move out, into the soil and the plants. I looked up and saw a woman, non-Caucasian, with white hair. I sang to her, then thought to ask who she was. She said she was a friend of my mother the Earth, and my mother was not well and needed me, needed us to sing to her every day to heal her.

Two years later my own mother was diagnosed with uterine cancer. I had not understood the very clear message about her being "not well," believing that the trance referred only to the Earth Mother. Fortunately my mother survived with the help of healing postures and rituals.

The sound of the Singing Shaman posture has been described as creating a tunnel through which the energy of the other dimensions can be channeled into this world. However, singing to the Earth, singing up the Sun, singing that the People may live, and singing as warriors preparing for battle may in turn send our own energy back to those living in Alternate Reality. One person said, "The sound created a bridge of light, which we could climb up and down."

Glossolalia is a vocalization that occurs in religious altered states of consciousness. Dr. Goodman's book on the subject of glossolalia, which was her own introduction to ecstatic trance, discusses the patterns of intonation and rhythm that characterize this phenomenon, which is known more commonly as "speaking in tongues." My own experiences of glossolalia all occur when I use this posture. My trance is usually very intense and I feel as though the sound overtakes my throat and my heart before my body begins to flow in the rhythm of the glossolalia. It is very beautiful, and I understand why people speak so blissfully of being possessed by the Holy Spirit when they speak in tongues.

DESCRIPTION

Again, this posture uses the standing position that is so common among the postures from horticultural societies. Stand with your feet about six inches apart, parallel and pointed straight ahead. Bend your knees slightly, eliminating any rigidity in your legs. Roll both hands slightly, as though you are

holding a small egg in the palm of each hand. Rest your hands gently on your chest, positioned so that the first joints of your little fingers touch at a point about midway along your sternum. Rest your upper arms close to the sides of the body, with no tension in your arms. With your eyes closed, tilt your head back slightly. Open your mouth, so that your jaw is completely relaxed. As soon as the rattling or drumming begins, start sounding an "aaahhh," like the vowel sound in "father." As the trance continues, allow, but do not force, any vocalizations as they occur.

APPENDIX

The special quality of a shared adventure is enhanced in a workshop. Workshops are scheduled each year at the Cuyamungue Institute near Santa Fe as well as around the United States and in Europe. Current listings of workshops in the United States and Europe can be obtained from the Cuyamungue Institute, Rt. 5, Box 358-C, Santa Fe, NM 87501. Certified teachers are also available to travel to communities where a group or individual may want to organize a workshop.

Introductory workshops focus on training the body to enter trance on cue, on teaching you to observe the subtle and dramatic changes in perception that accompany ecstatic trance, and on guiding your return to normal consciousness, again on cue. You are also training your mind to see and interpret the world in a different way. People living as hunter-gatherers or in a horticultural society grow up with an understanding of tribe or community. Their world, from which these ritual postures emerged, is not fragmented into categories such as physical, emotional, intellectual, social, and spiritual; rather, all are aspects of the whole, intricately woven together. In a workshop, as you learn to journey into Alternate Reality and share your experiences and listen to others describe their trances, you begin to appreciate that there are many ways to be a human being and to relate to other human and nonhuman beings, both in ordinary reality and in Alternate Reality.

The focus of an introductory workshop is to teach four or five commonly used postures, usually a sampling from the different categories. One workshop might include the Singing Shaman, a celebration posture; the Nupe Mallam, to introduce divination; the Sami Lower World posture, for an experience of a spirit journey; the Olmec Prince, to learn about metamorphosis; and the Bear Spirit, a healing posture that facilitates finding a new inner balance as the events of the trance experiences are integrated into both body and psyche.

Advanced workshops are designed for people who have become familiar with using ritual body postures to enter Alternate Reality and are ready to learn more about how to use the postures for specific purposes. For example, when I offer an advanced workshop on divination, I begin by defining divination and describing methods of preparing yourself to be a diviner. I review all of the divining postures to explain how each is best used. Then you use each of the divining postures, one by one. You frame your questions, enter trance, share your experiences, and learn to interpret what you have seen and heard in trance.

A different kind of advanced workshop may focus on the postures that have been discovered in one geographic area. The Olmec and Mayan cultures in Central America were rich with ritual body postures, and you can easily spend a weekend exploring their cultures as you learn the postures that have been discovered in Mexico and Guatemala. And there are many other ways creative teachers can combine sets of postures and design workshops for the needs of particular groups.

The centerpiece of ritual body postures and ecstatic trance is the Masked Trance Dance, a week-long workshop that recreates the ancient tradition of spiritual drama and ceremony. The workshop group lives together for the week, creating a working community while each person undertakes a very personal journey. This journey begins with a trip to the Lower World, to meet an animal spirit who will be your teacher and helper. Guided by further trance experiences, you create a mask and costume of this animal spirit. Then divination trances reveal the ceremonies of a ritual dance. The story of the dance is always different; however, it is usually a mythic story that is enacted in mask and costume, with drumming and singing, at dawn on the final day. It is a spiritual feast that nourishes each person and the community, bringing healing to the land where the Masked Trance Dance takes place. Dances are currently held in Ohio and New Mexico.

The Cuyamungue Institute has produced audiotapes of drumming and rattling for use in ecstatic trance. For information about ordering tapes, contact the Cuyamungue Institute, Rt. 5, Box 358-C, Santa Fe, NM 87501.

ENDNOTES

1. Erika Bourguignon, ed., *Religion, Altered States of Consciousness, and Social Change* (Columbus, OH: Ohio State University Press, 1973).

2. Felicitas D. Goodman, *Speaking in Tongues: A Cross-Cultural Study of Glossolalia* (Chicago: University of Chicago Press, 1972).

3. V.F. Emerson, "Can Belief Systems Influence Behavior? Some Implications of Research on Meditation," *Newsletter Review*, R.M. Bucke Memorial Society, 5:20-32.

4. Felicitas D. Goodman, *Where the Spirits Ride the Wind* (Bloomington, IN: Indiana University Press, 1990), p. 23.

5. B.W. Lex, "The Neurobiology of Ritual Trance," in E.d'Aquili, ed., *The Spectrum of Ritual: a biogenetic structural analysis* (New York: Columbia University Press, 1979).

6. John G. Neihardt, *Black Elk Speaks: Being the Life Story of a Holy Man of the Oglala Sioux* (New York: Simon & Schuster, 1959), p. 71.

7. Albert Hoffman, "The Transmitter-Receiver Concept of Reality," *ReVision: The Journal of Consciousness and Change,* 10:4, 1988, pp. 5-11.

8. Ingrid Mueller, unpublished research, University of Freiburg, Germany.

9. G. Guttman, C. Korunka, H. Bauer, and M. Leodolter, "DC-Potential Recordings During Altered States of Consciousness," *Research Bulletin* no. 27, Psychologisches Institut der Universitat Wien, 1988.

10. Elizabeth Marshal Thomas, *Reindeer Moon* (Boston: Houghton-Mifflin Publishers, 1987).

11. Richard Katz, *Boiling Energy: Community Healing Among the Kalahari Kung* (Cambridge, MA: Harvard University Press, 1982).

12. Marlo Morgan, *Mutant Message Downunder* (Lees Summit, MO: MM Co., 1991).

13. Felicitas D. Goodman, "Body Posture and the Religious Altered State of Consciousness: An Experimental Investigation," *Journal of Humanistic Psychology*, 26:3, 1986, pp. 97-98.

14. W. Lessa and E.Z. Vogt, eds., *Reader in Comparative Religion* (2nd edition) (New York: Harper & Row Publishers, 1965), p. 299.

15. Felicitas D. Goodman, "A Spirit Journey with the Priestess of Malta," *Eiddon Magazine*, 1992.

16. Goodman, *Where the Spirits Ride the Wind*, pp. 118-119.

17. Roberta Markman and Peter Markman, *The Flayed God: the Mythology of Mesoamerica* (San Fransisco: HarperSanFransisco, 1992), p. 5.

18. Neihardt, *Black Elk Speaks*, pp. 28-29, 36.

19. Goodman, *Where the Spirits Ride the Wind*, p. 107.

20. Felicitas D. Goodman, *Jewels on the Path: A Spirit Notebook* (Santa Fe, NM: The Cuyamungue Institute, 1990), pp. 86-91.

21. Goodman, *Where the Spirits Ride the Wind*, pp. 195-197.

22. Dennis Tedlock, *Popol Vuh: The Definitive Edition of the Mayan Book of the Dawn of Life and the Glories of Gods and Kings* (New York: Simon & Schuster, 1985).

23. Clarissa Pinkola Estes, *Women Who Run with the Wolves* (New York: Ballantine Books, 1992), p. 63.

24. Lessa, *Reader in Comparative Religion*, p. 299.

25. Carl Baynes, trans., *The I Ching or Book of Changes, the Richard Wilhelm Translation* (Princeton, NJ: Princeton University Press, 1950), p. xxiv.

26. Paul Linden, "Applications of Being in Movement in Working with Incest Survivors," *Somatics*, autumn/winter 1990-1991, pp. 38-47.

27. Michael Harner, *The Way of the Shaman* (New York: Harper & Row, 1980).

28. Johann Lehmer, ed., *Ecuador: Gold und Terrakotten* (Wien: Museum für Völkerkunde, 1990).

29. Markman, *The Flayed God*, p. 93.

30. Alfonso Ortiz, *The Tewa World: Space, Time, Being & Becoming in a Pueblo Society* (Chicago: University of Chicago Press, 1969).

31. Ignacio Bernal, *The Olmec World* (Berkeley, CA: University of California Press, 1969).

32. Thomas, *Reindeer Moon.*

33. Neihardt, *Black Elk Speaks,* p. 71.

34. Felicitas D. Goodman, *Jewels on the Path: A Spirit Notebook,* vol. II (Santa Fe, NM: Cuyamungue Institute, 1994), p. 55.

35. Goodman, *Jewels on the Path,* pp. 41-42.

36. Theodore Roszak, *The Voice of the Earth: An Exploration of Ecopsychology* (New York: Simon & Schuster, 1992), pp. 320-321.

37. Goodman, "The Nazca Lines: A New Hypothesis," *Jewels on the Path,* p. 54-63.

38. Harner, *The Way of the Shaman.*

39. Goodman, *Where the Spirits Ride the Wind,* p. 159.

40. Goodman, "The Venus of Galgenberg: A New Posture," *Jewels on the Path,* pp. 18-52.

41. Ibid., p. 40.

42. Felicitas D. Goodman, *Ecstasy, Ritual and Alternate Reality* (Bloomington, IN: Indiana University Press, 1988), pp. 32-33.

43. G. Baer, E. Ferst, and C.N. Dubelarr, "Petroglyphs from the Urumbamba and Pantiacolla Rivers, Eastern Peru," *Verhandl. Naturf. Ges. Basel,* 1984, 94:287-306.

44. Marija Gimbutas, *The Goddesses and Gods of Old Europe* (Berkeley, CA: University of California Press, 1982).

45. Goodman, "In the Land of Centaurs and Mermaids," *Where the Spirits Ride the Wind,* pp. 205-214.

46. Richard Bach, *Illusions: The Adventures of a Reluctant Messiah* (New York: Delacourt Press, 1977).

47. Ortiz, *The Tewa World,* p. 13.

48. Tedlock, *Popol Vuh,* p. 93.

49. Goodman, *Where the Spirits Ride the Wind,* pp. 192-194.

50. Felicitas Goodman, personal communication, 1991.

51. Leslie Gray with Carolyn Schaeffer, "Dr. Leslie Gray, Bridge Between Two Realities", *Shaman's Drum*, fall 1987, 10:21-28.

52. Goodman, *Where the Spirits Ride the Wind*, pp. 198-199.

ABOUT THE AUTHOR

Belinda Gore was raised in the Midwest, received a traditional education in psychology and public administration, and worked in women's health care and the Ohio correctional system before completing her doctorate and becoming a psychologist. She was trained in metaphysics in the United States and England in the 1970s.

In 1984 she met Dr. Felicitas Goodman, a religious anthropologist whose research is the foundation of the use of ecstatic body postures. Belinda is the vice-president of the Cuyamungue Institute, founded by Dr. Goodman, and teaches ecstatic trance workshops around the country.

Belinda and her husband John live in Columbus, Ohio, where she maintains a private practice combining psychotherapy with dreamwork, ecstatic trance, and, more recently, the use of the Enneagram as a guide to psychospiritual development.